The first time I called myself a Witch
was the most magical moment of my life.

MARGOT ADLER

About the Author

Ellen Dugan, also known as the Garden Witch, is a psychic clairvoyant who lives in Missouri with her husband and three children. A practicing Witch for over twenty-nine years, Ellen is an award-winning author of over a dozen books and a highly respected tarot reader.

Visit her website at www.ellendugan.com and her popular blog, "Blog of Witchery," at www.ellendugan.blogspot.com.

About the Artist

Mark Evans (Queens, NY) is an award-winning artist who has created storyboards, concept designs, and production illustrations for hundreds of clients around the world, including Coca-Cola, Walt Disney, and Marvel Comics. Visit Mark's website at www.cloudmover.net.

Mark would like to dedicate the art in this deck to the memories of his mother and father.

ELLEN DUGAN

WITCHES TAROT COMPANION

Illustrated by Mark Evans

Llewellyn Publications
WOODBURY, MINNESOTA

FIRST EDITION
Third Printing, 2014

Book design by Rebecca Zins
Cover design by Ellen Lawson
Cover background image © iStockphoto.com/Susan Trigg
Illustrations © 2012 by Mark Evans

Llewellyn Publications is a registered trademark of Llewellyn Worldwide Ltd.

ISBN 978-0-7387-2800-1
The Witches Tarot kit consists of a boxed set of
78 full-color cards and this perfect-bound book.

Llewellyn Publications
A Division of Llewellyn Worldwide Ltd.
2143 Wooddale Drive
Woodbury, MN 55125-2989
www.llewellyn.com

Printed in the United States of America

Contents

Introduction   1

My Tarot Journey   1

Symbolism: The Language of the Tarot   4

Performing a Witches Tarot Reading for
    Yourself   6
    *A Charm for Personal
        Meditative Readings   7*

Performing a Reading for Another   7

The Major Arcana   11

The Minor Arcana   79

Cups   81

Swords   125

Wands   170

Pentacles   214

Tarot Spreads   259

One-Card Reading   260

Three-Card Reading   261

Seven-Card Horseshoe Spread   262

The Significator Card Reading   263
Physical Appearance for Significator
Cards   264

Court Cards as Significator Cards:
Astrological and Elemental
Personalities   264
Astrological Signs for Significators   265

Elemental Personality Traits
for Significators   265

The Triple Goddess Spread   266

The Four Elements Spread   268

The Wheel of the Year Spread   270

Magick with the Witches Tarot Deck   271

Court Cards for Personal Magick and
Meditation   272
Calling on the Pages for Inspiration
and Enthusiasm   272

Other Spellcasting Options with
Court Cards   273
Kings' Verse   274
Queens' Verse   274
Knights' Verse   274

Tarot and Witchery   275

    Basic Directions   275

    Tarot Spell to Enhance Magickal
        or Tarot Studies   276

    Tarot Spell to Create a Strong, United Coven
        or Circle   277

    Tarot Spell for Abundance   278

    Tarot Spell for Protection   279

    Tarot Spell for Attracting Romance   280

    Tarot Spell to Heal a Broken Heart   281

    Tarot Spell for Hearth and Home   282

APPENDIX I: MINOR ARCANA NUMBER
AND COURT CARD MEANINGS   285

APPENDIX II: SYMBOLS IN TAROT CARDS   287

BIBLIOGRAPHY   299

ACKNOWLEDGMENTS   301

CONTENTS

Introduction

My Tarot Journey

*The road of life twists and turns
and no two directions are ever the same.
Yet our lessons come from the journey,
not the destination.*

Don Williams Jr.

I have been reading the tarot for over twenty-four years. How I first became interested in the tarot is a little unusual—some would even say unorthodox. So, did an old gypsy woman hand me a battered, faded tarot deck under the light of a full moon? Was I fascinated with the tradition and mystique of the cards? Was I captivated by their images and mysteries? Nope. That fascination and captivation came much later.

I started using tarot cards because it was a way to get folks to relax when I did clairvoyant readings. When I began working the psychic fair circuit, I was a young mother of three in my twenties. I used no props of any kind; I just turned on my tape recorder and focused on the client (classically called a querent), and then I asked to hold their hand and let it rip.

Of course, most people did not care to have me just sit there, some cocky twenty-four-year-old, holding their hand and strolling right through their heads... it caught them off-guard and, honestly, it frightened them. Scaring people was the last thing I wanted to do. With that thought in mind, I watched other readers and realized that the props—flashy tarot cards, candles, and the occasional (albeit cheesy) crystal ball—made their clients relax. We won't mention the readers that wore turbans (I kid you not).

Also, it was the early 1990s; back in the day at the local St. Louis psychic fairs, anyone *not* using cards was looked upon suspiciously. So, being practical, I went out, found a pretty tarot deck, and memorized those suckers. Just like flash cards, I memorized three basic keywords for each card at first, and that got me up and running. My husband used to sit and hold up a card at random while I fed our babies in their highchairs, so I could practice. And while my toddlers ran amok in my home, I memorized the tarot deck between laundry, dishes, diapers, and family duties. Once I had a basic idea of all seventy-eight cards, I started to seriously study. Typically this study happened during the kids' nap time or in the evenings when the kids were all in bed.

I found a few basic books on tarot that gave me more insight into the cards and their traditional meanings. I practiced performing readings on friends, and then my friends' friends. And then something wonderful happened: I realized that every card had a story to tell. Even before I was a published author, I always had a yen for a good story, and so I began to associate the cards with certain stories and/or people that I knew. Then I began to notice that certain cards falling in a specific position in the reading always meant the same thing, no matter who the querent was. Inspired, I began to use the cards as a springboard and to allow them to open the door to a more refined and detailed psychic reading.

I became thoroughly enchanted by the symbolism and magick in the cards. I found it fascinating, as a Witch, to discover that the suits of the tarot were not only based upon the four elements, but they shared the same basic qualities and meanings as well. The closer I looked at the cards, the more magickal symbolism I found. I began picking up different varieties of tarot decks to experiment with, and my affection and love affair with the tarot became stronger than ever before.

Over the past twenty years I have had a favorite basic tarot deck and a few funky ones, but I never had a tarot deck that felt magickal enough. I had a few Witch-themed decks, but they never truly fit me. Truthfully, they felt a bit tacky, or they were just too off the wall. Plus I found out quickly that folks would react negatively to those old, kitschy Witch-themed decks if I tried using them for public readings, which always made me want to giggle.

I wondered to myself if a strong, elegant deck with classic and beautiful images that Witches could identify with would ever come along. When the opportunity presented itself to design and script a brand-new tarot deck for Witches, well, I thought about it for about a day…and then started working. This Witches Tarot deck was a few decades in the wishing and over two-and-a-half years in the physical creation. However, I think you will find it to be worth the wait.

Symbolism: The Language of the Tarot

Symbolism is no mere idle fancy ...
it is inherent in the very texture of human life.

ALFRED NORTH WHITEHEAD

This deck is based on the classic Rider-Waite-Smith deck. If you are familiar with traditional tarot imagery, then you will pick up the basic definitions quickly. I do, however, strongly encourage you to take some time and read the descriptions of each card so you will understand the deeper magickal meanings displayed within them. Use this book to interpret the card meanings for yourself until you become familiar with their specific magickal meanings.

Every individual image portrayed in the scene of a single tarot card is there for a specific reason. Symbolism is the language of the tarot, and there are many different types of symbolism used in the Witches Tarot. It has always been my belief that each card tells its own wonderful story. I encourage you to look carefully at each card in this deck and see what tale it tells you. As you study the art of each card, read along in the book to discover what each flower, landscape, clothing color, jewel, tree, fruit, animal, or elemental creature represents.

Also, you will see that there are keywords of both upright and reversed meanings with each card definition. These will help you to learn the basic meaning of each card a bit more easily. Correspondences for deities as well as astrological and elemental associations are also listed where applicable. There is also a chapter on magick that features eleven new tarot spells. Also, be sure to refer to the two helpful appendices in the back of the book!

There is one appendix on the meaning of the numbers and the court cards of the Minor Arcana, and another detailed, alphabetized appendix on the common symbols employed in the cards. From a castle on a hillside to the thrones the characters sit in, right down to heraldry on the characters' costumes, I've got you covered. Now all of those symbols and their meanings are right at your witchy fingertips. All of these wonderful resources will help you, the tarot reader and/or Witch, to absorb and to learn the deeper meanings and the enchanting symbolism of the Witches Tarot.

Please note the design on the back of the cards as well, with their fantastic stars in the galaxy and the enchanting triple moon (which is, of course, our Triple Goddess symbol). What better symbol for the card backs in a Witches' deck could there be?

Embrace the magick of these cards, get ready to advance your skills, and enjoy the journey.

Performing a Witches Tarot
Reading for Yourself

*Reading is to the mind
what exercise is to the body.*

RICHARD STEELE

So, how do you begin, you may wonder? Honestly, it is really very simple. I suggest studying all of the images in the deck and reading through the symbolism and meanings to familiarize yourself a bit with this deck. Once you have done that, you are ready to begin. I personally like to center myself and find a quiet spot to put myself into a relaxed frame of mind. Sometimes I light a few candles or some incense to help get in the proper meditative state of mind. I make sure that the house is quiet and I will not be interrupted. It is my "me" time.

Doing a tarot reading for yourself is a form of meditation. I know that it always relaxes me, and I constantly learn something new. I encourage you to try it. Your personal readings overall will be much clearer and more enjoyable if you give yourself some meditative time.

Now that you are focused, centered, and calm, decide on your question. Here's a good tip: the simpler the question, the clearer the answer. Shuffle the deck, keeping that question firmly in mind. Choose your card layout, deal the cards, then live on the edge and read them.

Here is a charm to help you to focus. This will assist in easing you into a magickal state of mind for your own personal readings with the Witches Tarot.

Ꝛ Charm for Personal Meditative Readings

Created by a Witch to be used as a tool
There is wisdom here from the World card to the Fool.
With seventy-eight lessons and messages to receive
May I gain enlightenment; as I will, so mote it be.

Take your time reading and interpreting the cards. Enjoy yourself, and may you gain illumination. Blessed be.

Performing a Reading for Another

Each player must accept the cards life deals him or her:
but once they are in hand, he or she alone must decide
how to play the cards in order to win the game.

VOLTAIRE

Now, when it comes to performing a reading for another, there are some rules you should consider. As I am a practical Witch and an old hand at doing tarot readings for the general public, here are a few realistic and commonsense considerations when it comes to reading your Witches Tarot cards for another.

Ask if the querent/client has ever had a reading before. If not, then take that opportunity to explain what some of the more intense tarot images actually symbolize. This way, you avoid any frights or upsets from the client. For example, the Ten of Swords symbolizes being betrayed or stabbed in the back; the Death card shows change (and typically pops up in readings for pregnant women and people about to get married or head off to college, etc.—after all, their life is about to change forever and in a big way); and the Shadow Side card means facing your fears. So give the client reassurance before their very first reading begins. That way, you can both enjoy the experience.

Ask the querent what specific question they have at the beginning of the reading. Have them hold the question firmly in mind while they shuffle the cards. (Yes, your tarot deck may be handled by someone else.) It is best to have the querent/client shuffle and cut the deck themselves before the reading—that way, their energy and actions influence the cards and how they fall. There are some people who insist that you should never let another person handle your cards, but I prefer to let the client shuffle or cut the cards. An easy solution to this dilemma is that if you are doing readings for the public, then you may choose to have a separate deck strictly dedicated for public readings and another set of cards just for your own personal use.

You do not have to read reversed cards—unless you'd like to. I rarely do. Life is full of enough challenges. Besides, it does occasionally upset folks when they see upside-down cards. Whether or not you decide to read reversed cards is your personal choice.

Never predict death. Why? Well, odds are that you are wrong. Worse, what if you are wrong and someone decides to take you up on your prediction? In all the years I have done readings, I can count the number of times on one hand when the cards actually predicted an eminent physical death; each time it was in conjunction with someone inquiring about a relative who was in their final days, battling an illness of some kind.

Know your deck. It really kills the mood and makes you look unprofessional if you have to stop and look up the answers in the book during a public reading. So, if you are doing readings for the public, then know the deck cold. Be sure to take some time to learn the meanings and to practice before you read for the general public. However, if you are doing a reading for a close friend and they don't mind you interpreting their cards straight from the book, then sit back, relax, and have a great time.

Storing your tarot cards. Finally, when you are all through with your reading, your Witches Tarot cards do not have to be wrapped and/or stored in silk. The reason this folklore began is that silk deflects unwanted psychic vibrations—but this is not strictly necessary. If the idea appeals to you, then go for it. I typically place my tarot cards in a drawstring fabric pouch. It's practical—it keeps them clean and together, and it makes it harder to lose a card—and I have different fabrics and various colored drawstring bags for my different decks, so I can tell them apart quickly.

Remember that it is okay to laugh and have fun with a tarot reading. It is also perfectly fine to be more serious and thoughtful. Again, your personal style and your choices should be honored. We are all unique, and that difference gives our tarot readings personality and depth.

I think that about covers the basics. Enjoy yourself as you learn the deck and read this book. There are some brand-new tarot spreads for you to try out, as well as spells and magick. Let's begin our journey and explore the enchantment and mystery of the Witches Tarot.

The Major Arcana

*It is a fool's prerogative to utter truths
that no one else will speak.*

NEIL GAIMAN

The sequence of the twenty-two cards in the Major Arcana tells us the story of the Fool's journey. With the first card number, 0, we see the Fool begin his quest young, carefree, happy, and open to the experiences of his spiritual passage. By the time the Fool works his way through to the final Major Arcana card, numbered XXI, the World, our traveler is older, wiser, and has embraced the mysteries of his path.

A fascinating note is that the word *arcana* actually means "mystery." The scenes in the Major Arcana cards show us evocative images and archetypes. These archetypes are symbolic figures such as the Mother, the Father, the High Priest and High Priestess, and the Hero. They appear in various mythologies, religions, and mystery traditions from all over the world. These archetypal images in the Major Arcana are drawn from many magickal cultures. They are truly universal.

At any point in our lives we can embody a Major Arcana card, and we may feel as if we are living with the scene itself. These particular twenty-two cards appeal to our emotions and tug on our heartstrings. The imagery and archetypes within the Major Arcana link us all together, as they resonate on a deeper spiritual level. They speak to us by using the common language of emotion, a language everyone speaks.

When Major Arcana cards turn up in a tarot spread, they add weight and importance to the reading. These cards illustrate important spiritual matters, and they reveal our relationship to the particular archetype within the card. When two or more Major Arcana cards are dealt in a reading, then you know that fate is playing a hand in your spiritual path and everyday life. Take comfort in that, as these Major Arcana cards teach you that while things may seem beyond your control, there is a divine, magickal purpose at work here.

The Major Arcana offers you a road map to the mysteries of the Craft and to your spiritual life. All you have to do is be willing to open your eyes, embrace the offered wisdom, and start your travels. May you have a good journey!

0 • The Fool

The Fool is at the beginning of his spiritual and magickal journey. The Fool is young, open, and daring enough to take a risk and to make a leap of faith. He strolls along at the very edge of the cliff, a green valley below him and mountains at his back, either unaware or uncaring of the risk. He carries a leather satchel filled with his past experiences on his traveler's staff. These are kept safe and secure by his faith, symbolized by the pentagram that keeps the satchel closed. His bright, colorful costume gives a nod to both his happy mood and his sunny disposition. The red feather in his cap symbolizes his zeal for life and his love of the journey. The Fool has his face tipped up to the bright blue sky and is enjoying the freedom, excitement, and adventure of his journey.

The white rosebud that the Fool carries symbolizes his innocence, his trust, and those new beginnings. The dog portrayed in this card is the Fool's companion and familiar. It prances happily along beside him. West Highland White Terriers (or "Westies," as they are often called) are known for being loyal, energetic, and smart dogs—a perfect companion for the novice traveler.

Meanings

This first Major Arcana card is an excellent illustration of someone who is following their bliss. This card often materializes in a reading when the querent is trying something new and completely different. They may be just beginning their spiritual journey or are exploring a new magickal tradition or path. Perhaps they are taking on a brand-new job or are considering an innovative business opportunity. The Fool encourages us to dare, be more open minded, and enjoy the ride. Do not let yourself be dragged down by worries. The Fool laughingly persuades you to trust and take a chance, and not fret too much about the future—instead, just enjoy the trip and take things one day at a time.

This card is all about the proverbial leap of faith. Sure, it is possible that you might make a mistake or fall down, but hey! You can always get right back up, brush yourself off, and try again. Sometimes that is the best way to learn—by daring to do. At the end of the day, the Fool encourages you to be open to new prospects and ideas. Live on the edge; think outside of the box. Be confident and bold! There is a big, wide, magickal world out there…go explore it!

> *Keywords:* Follow your bliss. Adventure, fresh starts, exploration, a journey. New ideas; take a chance and chase your dreams. The beginning of a spiritual quest; exploring a new magickal path or tradition. A leap of faith.

> *Deity Associations:* None, because the Fool represents humanity.

> *Astrological Association:* Uranus.

> *Reversed:* Irresponsibility, recklessness, dangerous and careless behavior. A precarious situation. There is a need to be cautious and plan ahead.

The Magician stands behind an altar at dawn, with his pentagram around his neck and magickal symbols embroidered upon his robe. With the wand in his hand he draws a lemniscate, the infinity symbol, in the air above him, reminding us that "As within, so without." With his other hand he points down to the earth to illustrate another classic magickal proverb: "As above, so below." On the altar lie the classic Witch's tools, which are also the symbols of the four suits of the Minor Arcana: the cup to represent the element of water, the sword for air, the hawthorn wand for fire, and the golden pentacle for the element of earth.

The Magician is a commander of the four natural elements. By combining his personal power together with the natural elements, he makes magick through the sheer force of his will. He stands beneath a bower of red roses, which represents harmony. The four lilies in the foreground symbolize the purity of his relationship with deity and his creativity. The four faeries in the card represent each of the four natural elements: the green faerie for earth, red for fire, blue for water, and yellow for air. The faeries fluttering around the Magician's altar show us how he is intimately connected to and has a strong working relationship with the elementals and the awesome powers of the natural world.

Meanings

When this card appears in a reading, it is a message to tap into your own magick to find the answers you seek. Work in balance with the elements and the powers of nature to create your magick and bring about positive change. Magick is all around you, and it is everywhere in the natural world…the Magician challenges you to seek it out. Connect to this elemental energy and tap into its powers. Be confident and look within as well as without.

This particular Major Arcana card is a lesson in the Hermetic Principle of Correspondence, which teaches us that "As above, so below; as within, so without." We do exist on all planes—on the astral/spiritual, the energetic, and the physical. The Magician urges you to choose the most harmonious tools and natural accessories for your magick. Use the laws of correspondence and all of the resources that you have at your disposal wisely.

Keywords: As above, so below. Skill, determination, connection, confidence. Strength of will. Working magick with the four elements and the elemental spirits. The Hermetic Principle of Correspondence. Elemental magick and personal power.

Deity Associations: Hermes, Thoth, Mercury, Hermes Trismegistus.

Astrological Association: Mercury.

Reversed: Lack of confidence, poor communication with others, manipulative magick.

The High Priestess before you is powerful, mystical, wise, and compelling. She is serious, kind, just, and compassionate. This is the Maiden aspect of the Goddess, and her wisdom is all-encompassing. The High Priestess wears an ethereal silver gown and royal blue hooded cape as she sits in contemplation upon her throne, her feline familiar sitting calmly at her side. The blue sky and nature are her backdrop, and the moon and the stars of the cosmos are at her feet. Pomegranates grow lushly around her, and she is stationed evenly between the two lunar pillars. The High Priestess is calm and in control of the occult powers she wields. She does not lean towards the waxing energies or towards the waning energies of the moon, as she is not inclined to the light or the dark. The High Priestess is centered and neutral.

The High Priestess wears a Triple Goddess crown and a necklace of amber and jet stones to denote her rank. Amber increases mental power and jet enhances psychic abilities, both important qualities for the High Priestess. In her hands she holds a scroll for knowledge and blooming sage, which represents wisdom. The pomegranates are sacred to the goddess Persephone, and they signify royalty and elegance. The young black cat, the classic Witch's familiar, represents the feminine mysteries of the Craft.

Meanings

When this card appears in a reading, it often marks a time of initiation and learning. The Maiden Goddess is challenging you. Be wise and listen to her words of wisdom. This card is a reminder to quietly and calmly seek occult knowledge and look within. Use your intuition and trust your instincts. This is not the time to let your emotions rule you; instead, it is an opportunity for growth and a chance to gain real insight and understanding. The High Priestess teaches you to be strong, wise, and steady. She quietly shows you that in order to attain real wisdom you must remember to always work your magick thoughtfully and from a place of neutrality.

Keywords: The Maiden aspect of the Goddess. Neutrality, initiation, wisdom. Inner knowledge, intuition. Lunar energy and magick, waxing moon magick, the feminine mysteries of the Craft.

Deity Associations: Artemis/Diana, Persephone, the Maiden Goddess.

Astrological Association: Moon.

Reversed: Being out of balance. Repressed feelings, a refusal to learn and grow, unrecognized potential.

III • The Empress

The Empress is seated on a cushioned golden throne surrounded by nature. Her throne is embellished with patterns of five-petaled roses and wheat. The five-petaled flower creates a natural pentagram, and the flowers and sheaves of wheat link her back to the ancient mother goddesses Demeter and Isis. The Empress is pregnant in this card, indicating her fertility. She is the great Mother Goddess, and the twelve stars that form a halo around her head represent the signs of the zodiac. She holds in her hand a scepter, denoting her power over all of the natural world. The beautiful Empress wears a rich green gown, another link to the powers of life, growth, and nature. The nine pearls around the Empress's throat symbolize the nine classic planets, and pearls are a symbol for basic organic creativity.

A heart-shaped copper shield with a stylized Venus symbol rests to the side of her throne. This card has the astrological association of the planet Venus, and copper is the metal associated with that planet. The Empress's shield reminds us to protect and cherish the love in our lives. The lush forests, green grass, and the river that cascades down the slope are more depictions of sacred feminine symbolism. The background sky with the heavy gray clouds holds the promise of rain and life coming to the land. The wildflowers and wheat growing in the foreground of the scene correspond to the abundance of the harvest, and they represent prosperity and resources. Finally, the rabbit that sits contentedly at the Empress's feet is another nod to the energy and awesome powers of fertility, creation, and nature.

Meanings

This is the motherhood, fertility, and power-of-nature card. When this card appears in a reading, it is a message from the Mother Goddess to respect the force and power of nature and the body's ability to reproduce. If the Empress card appears in a reading along with the Ace of Wands or the Ace of Cups, then it symbolizes pregnancy or that conception may be likely at this time. This card can also indicate an opportunity to bring new, creative ideas into the world. Protect and cherish the loving relationships in your life. Focus on your family and your home, and enjoy the energy and excitement your children bring into your life. "Birth" your new ideas. Embrace creativity and your own sexuality, and work joyously and respectfully with the powers of nature.

Keywords: The Mother aspect of the Goddess. Bringing new ideas into existence. Feminine power, love, sexuality, motherhood. Fertility, birth, creativity. Hearth and home, protecting love in your life, full moon magick. The power of nature.

Deity Associations: Aphrodite/Venus, Demeter, Gaia, Isis, Inanna, Mother Nature, the Mother Goddess, Selene.

Astrological Association: Venus.

Reversed: Domestic problems, infertility, problems with parental or romantic relationships.

IV • The Emperor

The wise Emperor watches over his children as they play happily in the background. To denote his power, he holds a scepter topped by an ankh in his right hand. In his left hand he holds a globe. He wears a purple cape to represent his sovereignty. The mountains behind him symbolize his strength and steadfastness. The Emperor is surveying the scene and considering his options and plans for the future. He is a wise, kind ruler and a loving father figure. This card has the astrological association of Aries, which is represented by the ram's heads in the carved arms of the throne and the Aries symbol on the Emperor's armor.

This is the masculine characteristic of deity, the God aspect and the divine father. The purple tulips in the foreground symbolize royalty, while the blooming sorrel growing at his feet represents parental affection. Interestingly, the Emperor has no weapons and instead uses the power of his wisdom and experience to rule and to keep the peace.

Meanings

This card may symbolize a leader of a family or a magickal group—a responsible, balanced person. Just as the Emperor is doing in this card, you should calmly survey your situation and carefully consider your options. This card may stand for your boss at work (no matter what their gender), not just a husband or a father. The Emperor card will often appear in a reading when you are up for a promotion at work, about to earn a higher degree in your coven, or even if you are taking a new job with better prospects. If you find yourself standing as the head of the family or coven and are the peacemaker and arbitrator, it is possible this card may represent your role within the group. It can also symbolize your leadership within a family dynamic or at your place of employment.

Keywords: Leader of a family or coven. Father figure, family man, loving husband and/or father. Sovereignty, reason. Masculine energy, protection. A responsible and balanced person.

Deity Associations: Osirus, Zeus, Jupiter, Divine Father.

Astrological Association: Aries.

Reversed: Lack of self-discipline, authority issues, inferiority, issues with parents.

V • The High Priest

The High Priest sits on a stone bench at the temple. He is an elegant older gentleman, one of the Wise Ones. He wears a rich, flowing, regal scarlet robe, and his silver pentagram—a symbol of magickal power and personal protection—is displayed proudly upon his chest. The position of his right hand—two fingers up and two fingers down—and the wooden staff he holds in his left hand are classic tarot symbols. They represent balance between the worlds of the physical and the spiritual. The three crosspieces of the staff correspond to the upperworld, the middleworld, and the underworld.

In the background we see mountains and a lush natural setting. In the foreground a long shadow is cast. Two large skeleton keys hover in the air before the High Priest. These two prominent skeleton keys represent the divine feminine and the divine masculine, represented by the moon with its silver lunar key and the sun with its golden solar key, respectively. One of the many names for this card is the Hierophant. The High Priest is an authority figure, a counselor, and the keeper of magickal traditions and knowledge.

Meanings

When this card appears in a reading, it means that there are questions that need answering and advice to be sought. Classically this card denotes a need for legal advice or counseling. It may also indicate a course of study or furthering your education or the need to settle disputes in a coven. But remember that the High Priest is the wise and patient counselor, an elder, and a teacher. He does not give you all the answers to your questions;

instead, he helps you figure out where to look to find your own truths. He places in your hands the keys to unlock the mysteries and to gain deeper knowledge, then trusts that you will find the answers yourself, using the lessons he has so carefully taught you.

Keywords: Possible legal matters to attend to. Counseling, settling disputes in a coven, upholding tradition, preserving magickal wisdom. Understanding the mysteries of the Craft, furthering your education, uncovering your personal truths.

Deity Associations: Horus, Jupiter, Mithras, the Sage.

Astrological Association: Taurus.

Reversed: Receiving unreliable or unsuitable advice, making a hasty or poor decision, expecting others to make decisions for you.

VI • The Lovers

A pair of young lovers share an intimate moment in a beautiful spring garden filled with blooming trees, flowers, and a stream. Above and behind the couple, coming out of the clouds, an angel watches over the pair. The sun illuminates the winged angel, and the angel is reaching out and blessing the bond between the couple in a shower of beautiful, glowing light. Representing harmony and messages, the angel gently reminds us that love enlightens and heals.

The couple is on the verge of a kiss. Romance is in the air, and once the couple does kiss, their emotional commitment begins and their destinies will forever be entwined. They are about to discover whether they have chosen well.

The Lovers card is a card of choices made and romance. It is a wonderful illustration of the balance of opposites and the power of attraction. Classically the man represents reason and the woman symbolizes emotions. The woman wears a rosy-pink gown, the color of love and soft, happy emotions. She has six pink roses in her red hair; the six roses are a nod to the number of this card, which symbolizes a balance of opposites. Pink roses, in particular, stand for a romantic love. In bloom at the couple's feet are daffodils and hyacinths. These magickal flowers add the enchantment of chivalry and new love to the meaning of this card.

Meanings

The Lovers is a card of relationships and choice. This card illustrates the power of love, desire, destiny, romance, and attraction. It celebrates challenges overcome so that two lovers can be together. The angel in this Major Arcana card may be thought of as a matchmaker, but she may also be a protective force for the couple. The angel is a symbol of destiny. She is there to show us how every choice we make can affect our future. The angel reminds us to choose wisely.

Keywords: Sexual love, beauty, a romantic relationship. Decisions, commitment. Choices to be made. The choice you make now will affect your future. Love heals.

Deity Associations: Eros and Psyche, Isis and Osirus.

Astrological Association: Gemini.

Reversed: Relationship issues, poor choices made. Ignoring problems. Spats and squabbles.

VII • The Chariot

An armor-clad charioteer stands inside his gold and silver chariot as he races his horses through the clouds and across the sky. In the background we see a crescent moon, starry skies, and the sunrise's lighter sky beneath him. On the charioteer's helmet is an eight-pointed star. This is the star of Venus, a symbol of healing. Across his armor is a golden sash bearing the signs of the zodiac. He holds a magician's wand aloft in his left hand, and with his right hand he appears to be directing the two horses that are pulling the chariot with the strength of his will alone, as there are no reins on the horses. This illustrates that he is in control of his personal power and the magickal energy at play.

The Chariot tells the story of the Hero, he who has battled fiercely and won. This is the only card in the deck that has two horses in it, and their symbolism is important. This pair of horses mimics the pillars in the High Priestess card. To the driver's right is a black horse, which represents night, lunar magick, chaos, the subconscious, and feminine energies. The white horse on the driver's left symbolizes the day, solar magick, order, the conscious mind, and masculine energies. Rather than being ruled by those forces, the charioteer directs them and harnesses these powers to create the outcome that he desires—just as we see him controlling the pair of horses and keeping them moving forward together.

Meanings

This is a card that speaks of hard-won victories. The Chariot card is all about self-confidence, control, motivation, and the determination to succeed. Tap into your own personal power and you will see your goals manifest. Obstacles and blocks will be removed. Work magick for movement and change. When the Chariot comes roaring into a reading, it is a message to combine your magick with mental discipline and tenacity. Power comes from within. Believe in yourself—combine determination, focus, and willpower—and you will succeed. In the Major Arcana, only the Chariot, the High Priestess, and the Star cards have starry skies. These three cards are linked. If the High Priestess appears in a reading with the Chariot, it is a sign that victory can be obtained through wisdom. If the Star appears in a reading with the Chariot, it is a sign that the victory will bring an emotional healing.

> *Keywords:* Willpower, ambition, focus, drive. Leadership abilities. Tap into your personal power to see your magick manifest. Overcome adversity and any obstacles in your path. Don't give up; hang in there!
>
> *Deity Associations:* Apollo, Artemis, Helios.
>
> *Astrological Association:* Cancer.
>
> *Reversed:* No willpower, no drive, lack of focus or ambition, fear of commitment.

VIII • Strength

An auburn-haired woman sits quietly at dawn with a large male lion at her side. The lion is magnificent, and he leans contentedly into the woman for comfort. She is smiling, calm, and able to control the lion by her demeanor and touch alone. The woman is crowned with green oak leaves; these represent strength. A lemniscate—the infinity symbol — glows above the woman's head and shows that she is a spiritual and magickal being. Her gown is white and red; both of these colors are associated with the Goddess. Around her neck are eight glowing rubies. The number of these fiery stones is a reminder and a link to the number of her Major Arcana card. The necklace is an important symbol for the woman in the card, as the ruby is known for enhancing a positive and courageous state of mind. A garland of lush red roses, signifying harmony and beauty, drapes over the lion and the woman, linking them together—which brings up the question of who has strength in this card. The woman, for her quiet strength, power, and enjoyment of the situation? Or the lion, for being strong enough to tame his wilder impulses, to have self-control, and to allow himself the pleasure of the experience?

Meanings

Gentle strength, calmness, fortitude, and quiet personal power are the themes of this card. When this card turns up in a reading, it is a reminder that brute force is not necessary in the current situation; however, the wise use of personal power, self-control, determination, and strength of character are. Sometimes the strongest thing we can do is to have confidence in ourselves and our personal power—to be strong enough to work calmly and with determination through any challenges we may face, carefully and in complete control of ourselves.

Keywords: Strength of character, personal power. Restraint. Being calm. Self-control, confidence, determination.

Deity Associations: Apollo, Helios.

Astrological Association: Leo.

Reversed: Feeling helpless. Inhibition, fear, doubt. Control issues.

An old, wise wizard is on a vision quest. Perhaps he is Merlin; he has isolated himself, gone off alone, and has put himself to the test to uncover the mysteries. He wears a classic wizard's cloak covered with moons and stars, but the cloak is old, faded, and a bit ragged at the edges, showing us that he has been traveling for a while. Under the twilight sky a desolate snow- and ice-covered mountain range appears behind him, symbolizing his separation from the rest of the world. The Hermit uses his traveler's staff to help him on his journey. In his right hand he holds aloft an old metal lantern with a glowing six-pointed star held inside to light his way. A six-pointed star symbolizes the balance between masculine and feminine energies.

The Hermit's glowing star also reminds us to seek our spiritual truths both within and without. The star represents the wisdom that we all hold within. When this is allowed to shine forth, wondrous things can happen. If we have the strength, we can travel to the top of the mountain, gain insight, and see his light for ourselves. The Hermit gains experience through his trials and tests, and he reminds us that we can do the same. Knowledge, inspiration, and enlightenment can be ours.

Meanings

The Hermit card is all about taking purposeful time off, standing alone, and looking within. When this card appears in a reading, it is a sign that you need to take some downtime for yourself and regroup. Now is the time for vision questing, reflection, intuition, meditation, and self-development. It is time to work your magick solitarily for a while, even if you are a member of a coven. Trust in yourself and in your gut hunches, and take some personal time to see where this leads you. Let your magick light the way, no matter what challenges you are facing.

Keywords: Reflection, meditation, intuition. Taking time off from the coven. Solitary work, spending some time alone out in nature, gaining enlightenment.

Deity Associations: Hermes the Traveler, Saturn.

Astrological Association: Virgo.

Reversed: Feeling isolated or unable to cope with problems on your own. Loneliness. Time to seek out a new circle or coven.

silver, lunar pentagram is surrounded by the eight-spoked, golden, solar Wheel of the Year. In the background, we see bright blue skies and soft clouds. This card evokes the magick and mystery of the Wheel of the Year—all eight sabbats and the four seasons and cycles of nature.

The four seasons and their corresponding tarot suits are illustrated together. The earth element is represented by the pentacle and the winter solstice with holly, the classic Yuletide plant. In magickal herbalism holly is used for good luck and protection. In the bottom right we see pink cherry blossoms for the spring equinox together with the sword, which are both associated with the element of air. The cherry blossoms, a classic spring flowering tree, signify nobility and chivalry. In the bottom left corner there are vibrant green oak leaves for the summer solstice and the blooming hawthorn wand from our deck. Both the wand and the season of summer correspond beautifully with the element of fire. Here, the foliage of the midsummer oak represents health, wisdom, virtue, and long life. Finally, in the upper left-hand corner of the card, we see an enchanting mixture of beautiful orange maple leaves in the autumn combined with acorns for the harvest. The cups suit is aligned with the autumn season, as autumn is linked to the element of water. The maple leaves symbolize elegance, beauty, and energy, while the acorns bring prosperity and wisdom.

Meanings

This card symbolizes the magick of the four seasons and the energies of the Wheel of the Year. When this card turns up in a reading, it is a message to work with the energies and the cycles of nature that are currently around you, and not against them. This means rest and introspection in the winter; new beginnings, growth, and opportunities in the spring; energy, excitement, bounty, and vibrancy in the summer; and abundance and reminders to prepare, gather, and remember in the autumn. Expect there to be change, as all of life is forever transforming and growing. This card classically represents good luck, opportunity, and a fortuitous event.

> *Keywords:* The Wheel of the Year, celebrating the sabbats and esbats. Good luck. Working with the energies and magick of each season.

> *Deity Associations:* Fortuna, Arianrod.

> *Astrological Association:* Jupiter.

> *Reversed:* A period of bad luck. Feeling disconnected from the seasons and rhythms of nature. Seasonal affective disorder (wintertime blues).

The Greek goddess of justice, Themis, sits at her temple. She looks at you carefully with a direct, thoughtful gaze. Themis holds a double-edged sword in her right hand. The sword symbolizes that balance must be preserved, even if it is by force. In her left hand Themis holds the scales, also equally balanced. The emeralds in her crown and the emerald brooch pinned on her cape promote emotional stability and encourage wisdom. No one can see through the purple curtain behind her, as it conceals the mysteries and the inner workings of the universe.

This is the central card of the twenty-two Major Arcana cards, since Justice is at the center of our lives and she will have her impartial outcome. Themis treats all with integrity and reverence, as she is, in essence, a neutral force. Justice reminds us of the laws of karma and the idea of cause and effect. What we have done in the past and do now in the present will affect our future.

The Justice card illustrates equilibrium, balance, and fairness. It is time to weigh your options and to assess your actions in life. The black-eyed Susans growing in the Grecian urns elegantly symbolize justice in the language of flowers. The Justice card is connected to both the High Priestess and the Karma Major Arcana cards. Like the High Priestess, Justice is a neutral force, and its links to the Karma card remind us that, in the end, karma will always have its way.

Meanings

When the Justice card appears in a reading, you need to ask yourself what is out of balance and what sort of justice you are looking for. What is it that seems so unfair in your life? What actions of yours have brought you to this point? This card can represent legal matters and a possible court case. It can also symbolize a restoration of balance. It indicates that fair play, honesty, harmony, and balance are coming. Situations will work themselves out. Trust and leave the dispensing of this justice in the hands of the gods.

Keywords: Justice, legal matters, fair outcome to a court case. Cause and effect. Allowing the gods to take care of the outcome. Honesty, equilibrium, integrity, and equality.

Deity Associations: Athena, Ma'at, Themis.

Astrological Association: Libra.

Reversed: Bias, injustice, delays, unfair outcome.

XII • The Hanged Man

young man is calmly hanging upside down from his right foot on an ash tree. While he hangs there he is in a transitional state or undergoing an initiation of some kind. The halo around the Hanged Man's face shows him to be experiencing an epiphany. The peaceful skies in the background of this card tell you this phase is not a time to fear. You need to let go of something old and hurtful in order to gain this new wisdom. Enjoy this new perspective and in-between chapter of your life, and see what you discover.

In the Norse Pagan tradition, the world tree Yggdrasil supports the entire universe. The raven is a totem to the god Odin, and the bird symbolizes initiation, secrets, and prophecy. Just as Odin hung on the world tree to gain the knowledge of the runes, the Hanged Man also finds his answers on the ash tree during this transitional phase of life.

The raven holds a sparkling golden pentagram and looks down on the Hanged Man as if to ask what he is doing there. Perhaps this is his totem animal and it is keeping the Hanged Man company during his transitional state. Ravens are magickal, clever, and playful birds. They are attracted to sparkling and shiny objects and will cache them. The classic colors of red, green, yellow, and blue speak of balance within the four natural elements, and these colors make up the Hanged Man's costume. The runes embroidered around the neck of his shirt and decorating the trunk of the ash tree are a link back to Odin, the world tree, and the wisdom found there.

Meanings

When this card appears in a reading, it is a message to look at things from a different viewpoint. Embrace the idea of initiation as a vehicle to newer wisdom and a clearer spiritual path. Let go of the illusion of control, turn things on their heads, and look carefully at the lessons before you. Relax and be patient; this may not be easy, but fighting against the changes in your life only creates more drama. Read the signs carefully, be they tarot cards or runes. Meditate on their lessons as you allow yourself to go through this transitional or initiatory phase calmly and with joy. By doing so, you will uncover the mysteries.

> *Keywords:* Initiation, transitional phase of life. Relax and let changes come. New outlook on life, rune magick, gaining a new perspective on a current situation.

> *Deity Association:* Odin.

> *Astrological Association:* Neptune.

> *Reversed:* Being stuck, not being able to let go or move forward.

XIII • Death

The Death card is one of the most misunderstood cards in the tarot deck. Rarely does it symbolize physical death; instead, what it announces is radical change in the querent's life. In this card, Death's skull is lit with a glowing fire. The skull is a symbol of human mortality, and it is the seat of the mind. The greenish-yellow flames represent the mind's energy and power. Death's armor is dark and well used; his white horse has glowing eyes and a bridle with skull-and-crossbones trim. Death carries a flag that announces transformation. The flag is emblazoned with the number thirteen—the number of full moons in a year—and the flower on the flag is a five-petaled white rose, symbolizing the natural cycles of life. The brilliant red skies of sunset in the background correspond to the close of the day and the close of one chapter in your life.

A child stands before Death with an offering of a bouquet of white daisies bound together with ribbons in the Triple Goddess colors of white, red, and black. In the language of flowers, white daisies symbolize innocence. It is important to note that the child is looking up and facing Death while holding out the flowers. He is happy, trusting, and unafraid of this knight; he welcomes the change. The child represents hope.

Meanings

This card represents change. In order for something new to grow, something old has to give way. This card often shows up in readings for pregnant women, which makes sense. Think about it: their way of life is about to change forever. Their lives are about to transform into something else new and exciting.

This card also symbolizes other important endings and beginnings in your life: birth, marriage, new job, leaving for college, moving, etc. Basically, one way of life is gone, allowing room for new beginnings and opportunities to emerge.

Keywords: Transformation, change. Endings and beginnings. Cycles of nature and of life.

Deity Associations: Hades, Pluto, Hel.

Astrological Association: Scorpio.

Reversed: Traumatic adjustment, delay, difficult change.

The Greek goddess of the rainbow, Iris, faces forward and stands at the edge of the water, her golden wings outstretched. Her sheer white gown has a golden triangle on the bodice, which signifies balance and creativity. Her gown flows softly around her, and one of Iris's feet is on land while the other dips in the water. Neither on shore nor in the water, she is in an enchanted location where she is in both worlds—an in-between place.

In Iris's hands are two different goblets, and she calmly pours water from one goblet into another. The water flows magickally out and about before ending up in the bottom goblet. There is an alchemical transformation taking place here; she is tempering the liquid in the goblets to find the right balance, or mixture. Behind Iris, the clouds have parted in the sky and a rainbow appears, representing hope, magick, and miracles. Around her on the green banks grow iris flowers in several different colors. The enchanting iris flowers symbolize "an eloquent message," which suits the messenger goddess they were named after.

Meanings

The Temperance card appears in a reading when it is time to be restrained, to be a little more tactful than usual, and to employ some moderation. This Major Arcana card represents the mixing of different magickal elements to create something new, like rain and sunlight make a rainbow. The Temperance card also stands for the personal alchemy of a spiritual transformation. Now is the time to work on the healing of your spiritual self.

This the perfect occasion to work on finding the correct balance, or "flow," in your magick and your life. Watch for messages from the gods.

> **Keywords:** Alchemy. Restoring equilibrium. Moderation, restraint, and tact. Find your balance, look for divine messages, and work on spiritual healing and transformation.

> **Deity Associations:** Iris, Hebe.

> **Astrological Association:** Sagittarius.

> **Reversed:** Behaviors and actions that are out of balance. Addiction.

The Shadow Side replaces the traditional Devil card; Witches don't identify with the concept of a Devil figure. The Shadow Side shows what happens when you let fear and panic take over. The card illustrates a couple cringing away from a shadowy and frightening figure. They are alone in a sinister forest. Clearly their fear is ruling them. The clothes of the man and woman are dark and dreary, representing their unhappiness at being in a dark place in their lives. The posture and expressions of the couple illustrate their fear and show that they have inadvertently given away their power to someone or something else. Running and hiding from the shadowy creature is not helping the couple, nor are they finding any comfort. Instead they must turn and face their fears, and stop letting situations and people frighten, intimidate, or upset them.

We all must walk through dark times now and again. The question is, are you going to rise to the occasion and defeat your fears? Will you face the challenging people in your life and deal with the situations head-on, or will you whimper and fret about it? Face your adversaries and fight back with honor and integrity, and you will defeat those who challenge you.

Meanings

This card symbolizes that you are allowing someone else or a situation to have power over you. The old coven-mate who left in high drama, the in-law from hell, or the boss you cannot please—this is a person who can walk into a room and ruin your day... because you let them. Break those chains and walk out of the shadows! Stop giving away your power, and stand strong. What is important to remember is that you can break free of your reaction anytime you wish. It's time to embrace the shadow side of your personality and to really look your fears in the face. Come to terms with whatever is holding you back. Stop cowering. Work to find balance and courage.

Keywords: Allowing another person to have power over you and your reactions. Defending yourself from baneful magick. Overcoming fear to emerge victorious.

Deity Associations: Pan, the Horned God, Volos.

Astrological Association: Capricorn.

Reversed: Oppression, illusions, trickery, deceit.

The Tower card illustrates that there has been a dramatic revelation or a sudden change of plans. Stormy, dark skies surround a tower that sits high on a cliff. Lightning snakes down from storm clouds and strikes the tower, knocking a crown off the top. Within the tower a fire burns, which cleanses and transforms. Two figures fall from the tower, and they are tumbling headfirst. This shows us that this event is completely out of their control.

The tower symbolizes our ambitions, while the ruby-studded crown represents the ego. In magickal traditions, rubies are used to intensify awareness. The lightning bolt in this scene represents that there is now a flash of insight, and the bright light of truth will illuminate any questionable situation. Blocks are being removed, and negative energy is finally being broken through. Transformation is occurring; reevaluation is necessary at this time. You are being forced out of your comfortable little world…now you will have to deal with the aftermath.

Meanings

The Tower card is all about a shocking revelation or an event that forever changes the way you see yourself and the people around you. This is not necessarily a negative thing. Now that all of that built-up pressure has been released from the tower, the fire inside will both cleanse and transform it. Shocking secrets are uncovered; you may take a blow to the ego, but you will survive your tumble. Change is coming, and it's going to be dramatic. The spiritual blocks or obstacles you once faced are now removed. What you learn will end up being helpful in the long run.

Keywords: Change of plans, revelation of secrets. Upheaval. A blow to the ego. Situations coming to a head. Reevaluation. Dramatic change. The removal of blocks in your spiritual path.

Deity Associations: Mars, Thor, Zeus.

Astrological Association: Mars.

Reversed: Arguments, trauma, frustration, destruction.

The Star Goddess stands nude at the water's edge. One of her feet is on land, while the other is in the water. Her arms are held out over both the water and the land. She holds simple pottery jugs in each hand. One stream of water flows down to the earth, representing physical healing, while the water from the other jug flows back into the pool of water, symbolizing spiritual healing. A large star shines in the night-time sky, surrounded by seven smaller stars. Each star has eight rays shimmering out from it. The eight-rayed star is a symbol of healing, and it is an emblem of the goddess Venus, whom the evening star was named after. The glowing stars depicted in this card remind you to follow your dreams, to work with the quiet tides and energies of the stars, and that wishes will be fulfilled at this time. Around the Star Goddess and on the banks grow blue forget-me-nots. The forget-me-not flowers, also sacred to the goddess Venus, represent hope and love.

Not unlike the Temperance card, the Star Goddess is working between the worlds in this depiction. To be "between" is one of the most magickal of places. The sacred ibis bird standing on the log at the shore represents Thoth, an Egyptian god of divine wisdom and science. Thoth was the inventor of astronomy and was considered patron to the art of magick.

Meanings

The Star is a card of hope, inner peace, creativity, and healing. When this beautiful, tranquil card turns up in a reading, it is a sign that physical and emotional healing is on the way. Have hope, follow your dreams, and your wishes will be granted.

This card speaks of inspiration; your creativity will flow better than ever before. Let it fill you up, and see where it leads you. The Star illustrates a softer, gentler magick and indicates that you will be working successfully with your intuitive gifts. Also, astrological timing is imperative to any magick performed at this time.

> **Keywords:** Healing, inspiration, intuition, renewal. Hope, peace, wishes granted. Astrological magick. Wisdom. Creativity is flowing.

> **Deity Associations:** Star Goddess, Astrea, Venus, Isis, Ishtar, Nuit, Thoth.

> **Astrological Association:** Aquarius.

> **Reversed:** Pessimism, delay, doubt, spiritual blocks.

ecate the Crone stands at the foggy crossroads, holding a torch aloft. Her silver hair flows out on a breeze; around her throat she wears a Hecate's Wheel pendant. At her waist hang three skeleton keys and a pentagram. Hecate Trivia, "the goddess of the three ways" or the goddess of the crossroads, held sway over the earth, the sky, and the sea. She could appear in any number of guises—as a beautiful maiden, a matron, or as the crone and guide, as she is depicted here. A crone is a woman of power—a woman who has acquired great knowledge in her lifetime, who walks with wisdom, and who wears her years beautifully.

Hecate's trio of companion wolves represent the wilder aspects of ourselves. Hecate was always accompanied by canines, both wild and domestic. The two willow trees in the background are sacred to Hecate, and the willow corresponds both with the element of water and with lunar magick.

Hecate shows us that there is more to be seen than we would first imagine, such as a crone who is beautiful instead of haggard and wizened. Magick is everywhere, even in the most unsuspecting of places. Look carefully now—what will Hecate and the light of the moon reveal to you?

Meanings

This is the card of the Crone Goddess, waning moon magick, intuition, and illusions. It may also represent a development of psychic powers. When this card appears in a reading, it reveals that people and situations are not always as they appear. The moonlight can be deceptive. What looks one way during the day may appear completely different under the shifting light of the moon. You need to look carefully at what you think you see. Call on your guides, totems, and Hecate to see past the fog and to recognize the truth. Use your psychic gifts and trust your intuition. Work magick with Hecate now to see through any illusions and for the gifts of foresight, wisdom, and protection.

Keywords: The Crone aspect of the Goddess. Waning moon magick. Protection magick. Seeing through what others would keep hidden. Intuition and the development of psychic powers. Wisdom gained through years of life experiences.

Deity Associations: The Crone, Hecate Trevia, Hekate.

Astrological Association: Pisces.

Reversed: Confusion, deception, deceit, anxiety, fear.

XIX · The Sun

A young blond boy is riding a white horse through a field of gorgeous sunflowers. Above him, in a summer blue sky, white clouds are illuminated by the brilliant sun that radiates down. It is the height of the growing season and a day of power: the summer solstice. The little boy portrayed in the card is sweet, smiling, happy, and having an adventure. He embodies excitement, enthusiasm, and joy. If you listen carefully, you will hear him call you to come join him on his adventure. He is the divine sun child.

Sunflowers naturally turn to face the sun during the day, and in the language of flowers the sunflower symbolizes fame, success, and esteem. The white horse stands for movement and progress. In many mythologies a white horse represents the dawn, life, light, and illumination. Also, white horses are linked to magick and the Faery realms. The white horse, the blond child, and the sunflowers are all recognized as classic solar symbols. This happy Major Arcana card is also associated with personal power and the celebration of the equinoxes and the solstices.

Meanings

This is one of the most fortuitous cards in the tarot deck. The Sun is a card of good omens, good luck, achievement, creativity, and breakthroughs. Dance under the light of the sun and work some solar magick. Success is yours; expect happier times, good health, energy, and vitality. Spiritual wholeness has been achieved. You will enjoy good times with dear friends, and magickal events and celebrations are coming your way. Personal power is at its peak. Focus that charisma and see where it takes you. Things are working in your favor, so hang on tight and enjoy the ride!

> **Keywords:** Achievement, personal power, good times, happy events. Friendship, vitality, joy, enthusiasm. Fame, growth, success, happiness. Solar magick. The solstices and the equinoxes.

> **Deity Associations:** The Sun Child, Apollo, Brigid, Helios, Sunna.

> **Astrological Association:** Sun.

> **Reversed:** Needing to come back to reality. Competition. The demands of being in the public eye.

XX • Karma

The people have joined hands and are raising them in celebration as they look up at the totality of a solar eclipse. They are a family unit: a woman, a man in the center, and their child. The family has gathered for a celebration of the eclipse. They stand before a magick circle where torches help to light their ceremonial area. The trio wear ritual robes with purple sashes. Purple is powerful and it is both a spiritual and an intuitive color—a good choice for this card. In the distance are a green field and mountains. Those mountains are a classic symbol for this card and are believed to represent abstract thoughts. The light is strange, as, with the eclipse occurring, it is both day and night.

The eclipse reminds us that forces greater than yourself are at work here. The full solar eclipse traditionally indicates miracles and magick, and it is an enchanting reminder that deity is at work in your everyday life. Everything happens for a reason. Now you must come to terms with your past experiences. Ask yourself what lessons you have learned from them. This way, you can gracefully proceed with a greater understanding.

Meanings

The Karma card shows us that cycles and change have to be respected and that everything happens for a reason. Honor the changes in your life and grow with them. There are spiritual forces at work. It is time for you to make an important decision. Your destiny will be shaped by the choices you make today; keep in mind that the karma to follow will be of your own making. So be aware of both your actions and your magick on a spiritual level. Karma always has its way. Work consciously to create a positive transformation.

Keywords: Making a positive change for your future reality. Renewal, deeper spiritual and magickal awareness, karma and destiny. Reflection on past events. Results of your past actions.

Deity Association: Horus.

Astrological Association: Pluto.

Reversed: Bad judgment, regret. Feeling the unfortunate consequences of the magickal rule of three. What goes around comes around.

The World card symbolizes the end of the Fool's travels and is a culmination of all the cards before it. He has worked his way through the mysteries of the Major Arcana and has found completion. The Fool is shown in the upper left-hand corner. He is older and wiser now that he has completed his magickal journey. In the other three corners of the World card we have representations of the gifts he has acquired while on his expedition. In the upper right-hand corner, a golden eagle soars through the sky. The eagle stands for the gifts of intelligence, courage, and confidence. In the lower right, we see an adult male lion. The lion signifies the gifts of strength, passion, and rebirth that the Fool has now obtained. In the lower left-hand corner is a powerful stag. The stag symbolizes pride, poise, and integrity. Our wiser and older Fool can now easily put to use all of these skills both in his magick and in his daily life.

The Green Man in the center of the World card smiles out at us with foliage surrounding his face and branches crowning him. The branches coming from the top of the Green Man are a nod to the antlers of the horned god of nature. For Witches, the Green Man is a beautiful and evocative representation, or archetype, of the awesome powers and magick of the natural world. It is a perfect representation for the final card of the Major Arcana, as the Green Man and the World card are both symbols of renaissance, rebirth, and regeneration.

Meanings

When this card appears in a reading, it is a sign that spiritual lessons have been mastered. There is a sense of freedom and harmony to be enjoyed. Newly acquired knowledge, strength, and even spiritual understanding will now be put to good use. It may also symbolize successful completion of a project, a personal renaissance, or even strong and healthy spiritual connections between people and/or coven members.

Keywords: Rebirth, wholeness, completion, joy. Victory and achievement. A journey's successful end. The magick and wonder of the natural world. Spiritual connections between people and/or coven members.

Deity Associations: The Green Man, Gaia.

Astrological Association: Saturn.

Reversed: Delayed completion of a project. Recurring problems. Turning your back on the magick of the natural world.

The Minor Arcana

In the tarot, as in magic,
the four emblems stand for
the world itself and for human nature...
RACHEL POLLACK

The Minor Arcana consists of four different suits: cups, swords, wands, and pentacles. Each of these suits aligns with one of the four natural elements. Many tarot readers forget that the suits are, in fact, based upon the four elements. In this deck the elements are prevalent and affect the situation in each card.

In the Minor Arcana and within each of the four suits there are two different sets of cards. To begin, we have "the pips," or numbered cards, the ace through ten. The second set of cards in the Minor Arcana are the court cards—these being the page, the knight, the queen, and the king. In the Witches Tarot deck, each of the court cards has an enchanting personal message, challenge, or lesson for you, so read them carefully.

The suits of wands and swords are considered to have masculine energies assigned to their respective elemental rulers of fire and air. These suits are considered active, while the suits of cups and pentacles are feminine. The water and earth suits are passive.

It is also interesting to note that, in readings, the suits of pentacles (earth) and wands (fire) represent physical activities, while the suits of cups (water) and swords (air) symbolize the emotions that are being felt. The different elements characterize not only different experiences but also very different ways of approaching the challenges in your life.

Modern tarot decks based on the Rider-Waite-Smith deck follow the Golden Dawn standard, as does this deck. That is to say, they assign the element of air to the swords and the element of fire to the wands. While it may seem reversed to modern-day Witches, this is classic imagery. For this deck I wanted the card images to have a witchy flair, with images and meanings that are easily recognizable to avoid confusion. This way, the card reader will be able to easily flow with their readings.

While doing a reading, it is distracting to have to pause, look at a card, and wonder, "Wait a minute—what card is that?" Or, worse, to have to waste time or ruin the flow of the reading while you search your memory for a more familiar or classic image of a card, and then transpose the definition onto the deck you are currently using.

In closing, the Minor Arcana—both pip and court cards—shows us the everyday, ordinary situations and personalities that we deal with and face in our lives. The Minor Arcana cards bring meaning to events and clarity to the challenges we face, and provide illumination to the common questions we ask.

Cups

Life's enchanted cup sparkles near the brim.

LORD BYRON

The suit of cups symbolizes the element of water and all the magickal associations that flow from this element, such as psychic abilities, love, and emotion. Cups cards flow down a path to understanding through love, inspiration, and imagination. This suit illustrates the power of emotions, friendship, family, romance, and relationships. It explores how we are connected to each other. The element of water, in all its many forms, is celebrated in this suit—from misty, rainy skies to ponds, fountains, calm lakes, rivers and streams, waterfalls, gorgeous beaches, and moody oceans. Plus we'll meet a few of the magickal creatures who dwell there. The elemental beings associated with cups and water are the mermaids, and they do make an appearance in this suit. Some of the creatures aligned with the element of water are also depicted in the suit of cups— look for dolphins and a fish with a secret.

There are also plants, trees, flowers, and their respective magick incorporated in the card images. The flowers shown in the cups suit are associated with the element of water, such as foxgloves, water lilies, iris, violets, pansies, and roses. There is also a lunar pumpkin and a willow tree, both associated with the element of water as well. Each of their messages is explained in the individual meanings of their cards.

The suit of cups is aligned to people born under a watery zodiac sign: Cancer, Scorpio, and Pisces. Physically the court cards of the cups suit represent people who have light brown to blond hair and blue or green eyes. In addition, individuals who are drawn to the cups suit may be romantic, sensitive, psychic, and very empathic, and they may let their emotions lead the way. They are the dreamers and the mystics of the world.

Ace of Cups

The Ace of Cups floats on the surface of a shimmering lake at dawn. The silver cup with a stylized scallop design is surrounded by blooming pink water lilies and green lily pads. The cup is overflowing with water all on its own, and there are four streams of water—one for each direction and element—spilling over the edge of the silver cup and back down into the lake, returning the water to its source. In the background the sun rises over the brim of the cup, signaling the birth of a new day. The feminine element of water is the focus of this card. The cup, or chalice, is a time-honored symbol of the Divine Feminine. The cup is thought of as the womb from which all life flows. This particular ace is an auspicious card for personal relationships, as this suit is aligned with love and emotions. The Ace of Cups also symbolizes opportunities that come out of the blue and emotional growth and the gifts that come with it. The Ace of Cups tells us that the time is now for new and creative projects, divine inspiration, a new romance, a new life, and fresh starts.

Meanings

The Ace of Cups is the most potent and pure form of the feminine element of water. When the Ace of Cups appears in a reading, it proclaims birth, growth, love, and clairvoyance. This card often appears when a pregnancy is about to be announced or confirmed. However, there is more to the Ace of Cups than just physical birth. It does symbolize a wedding, a happy marriage, a healthy relationship, and a loving family. It may also be a symbol for emotional growth and healing. Remember, too, that the element of water is associated with psychic powers, creativity, imagination, and spiritual and emotional fulfillment. Gaze into the surface of that overflowing silver cup … what new, enchanting things are about to be birthed into your world?

Keywords: Births, weddings, happy news and celebrations. Romance and relationships. An emotional beginning. Psychic powers, creativity, and healing. The element of water.

Reversed: Selfishness. Your ego is getting in the way of your success.

man and woman stand before a beautiful, calm, and sparkling lake. They are facing each other and are smiling and happy. The woman's gown is ocean blue and has long, flowing sleeves. The man's clothes are watery shades of blue and green in a nod to the ruling element of water that the cups card represents. With their front hands they are each holding out a silver cup and toasting each other. Their back hands are bound together at the wrists with a golden cord, symbolizing that they are handfasted. Where the rim of the silver cups touch, there is a bright, glowing light radiating out.

Both the man and woman have a chaplet, or wreath, of flowers in their hair, made of violets, white roses, white and purple pansies, and deep green ivy. The violets are sacred to the goddess Venus, and these flowers speak of a faithful lover. The white roses in the couple's chaplets symbolize new beginnings and true love. The cheerful pansies tell us that the couple shares loving thoughts, and the ivy represents the fidelity of marriage vows held sacred.

Meanings

The Two of Cups represents relationships specifically between two people. This card symbolizes balance and equality. Here is a magickal union that binds together heart, body, and soul in the best possible way. When this card sails into a reading, it symbolizes romance, an engagement, or a happy marriage or romantic relationship. This card may also be a sign of an upcoming wedding or handfasting ceremony, depending on the cards that fall around it, such as the Four of Wands. The Two of Cups may also indicate a close friendship or successful and happy business partnership. It illustrates the hope of a new journey together as a couple and shows us that there are always new emotional opportunities for supportive friendship as well as a true and lasting love.

Keywords: Romance. An engagement, handfasting, wedding, or reconciliation. A partnership. Equality and true love.

Reversed: Problems in your relationship. Arguments, quarrels. Separation or divorce.

Three of Cups

coven of three women are grouped together and facing each other. Each woman holds up a silver cup as if they are celebrating and toasting their group's success. To further reinforce the element of water and its magick, we see a flowing waterfall and stream in the background. The women are wearing flowing, colorful gowns with mystical symbols on them, and their magickal silver jewelry sparkles in the sunlight as they appear to be quietly celebrating a sabbat, perhaps Midsummer, in the garden.

The trinity of women are surrounded by many different kinds of magickal flowers. Each of the flowers in this card are associated with the element of water. The tall, rosy-purple foxgloves represent Faery magick and protection. The irises whisper of magickal messages and the communication that flows between the coven members. The pansies, also known as heart's ease, show that they all think kindly of each other, while the violets are blessings from the Goddess and the faeries. Finally, the pink roses announce a real and lasting friendship. This card illustrates the power of three, and there are three trinities in the card: the three women, the three cups, and the three tall spires of the magickal foxglove plant.

Meanings

When this card flows into a reading, it is a reminder of the bonds of magick and friendship, and it is an illustration of the power of three. Your magick is manifesting at this time, whether you have cast your spells as a solitary or with your beloved friends and members of your coven. Magick is all around—and it is working. Expect growth, success, and creativity. Your goals are coming to fruition. This card represents a magickal friendship that brings delight and enchantment into your life. It may also indicate spiritual or psychic growth, gaining a new degree in your coven, or advancing in your course of magickal studies.

> *Keywords:* A happy occasion. A gathering of friends, family, or coven members to celebrate. The power of three and the magick of manifestation. Observing the sabbats, sharing experiences. Magickal advancement, psychic growth, the bonds of a healthy magickal friendship. Growth, success, creativity.

> *Reversed:* Self-centeredness. Strife within the coven. Your magick has come up against roadblocks.

Four of Cups

A young boy sits on the banks of a lagoon, sulking beneath a weeping willow tree. A waterfall is in the background. While it may be a beautiful day, with blue skies and puffy clouds, the boy's arms are crossed over his chest and his head is down. In front of him sit three silver cups, and he seems to be brooding about them. Off to the boy's side, a blue-eyed mermaid with platinum-blond hair is holding a fourth cup, and she is lying out in the surf. The pearls in her hair and around her wrist are associated with the lunar and feminine energies, and they represent dreams of what yet may be. The elemental mermaid is fair, whereas the boy is dark, and they are a contrast—however, they have very similar expressions. Perhaps she is mimicking the boy's expression in the hopes of teasing a smile out of him? The mermaid waves her gorgeous blue- and green-striped tail up and behind her, patiently waiting for the boy to look up and see the opportunities within his reach—to accept the help that she is trying to offer him. The willow tree in this card is associated with the moon and the element of water. In the language of flowers, the willow represents patience.

Meanings

This card illustrates boredom and feeling stuck in a rut or dissatisfied with your life. However, adventure, change, and assistance are being presented to you—you just need to open up your eyes to discover and perceive those new, enchanting possibilities. Help is coming from an unexpected place. Snap out of it! Be thankful for the blessings in your life and reevaluate where you currently stand.

> *Keywords:* Snap out of the funk you are in! Change, adventure, and opportunity await you. Quit moping and do something positive. Assistance is coming from an unexpected place.

> *Reversed:* Self-pity, self-indulgence, depression.

Five of Cups

A beautiful elemental creature, a mermaid, is on the shore, sitting on rocks. She is moody, dangerous, intense, and clearly bored with her world. Her hair and scales are a deep, intense, shimmery turquoise color. The sea seems to be taking on the temperament of the mermaid and is also a cloudy and dark blue-green. The surf is hitting the rocks behind her, showing her turbulent mood, and around the mermaid is a collection of her treasures from the sea. The gold coins are unnoticed, and her lunar crown of pearls brings her no joy. There are five silver cups in front of her, and while two of the cups are upright, three have tipped over and are spilling water out and back into the sea. The mermaid looks unhappy, as if her treasures no longer bring her pleasure. Like the classic folktale of the mermaid who longs to be on land and leave her watery kingdom behind, this mermaid has turned her back on the sea and is longing for something she cannot have.

Meanings

This card symbolizes dissatisfaction, being pessimistic, and yearning for something you can never have. Out of the five silver cups that are presented in this card, two of the cups are still full. It is interesting to note that most people only notice that three of the cups have spilled their contents out. When this card washes up in a reading, it is a warning that boredom, minor disappointment, and moodiness are taking over your life. You are wanting what you cannot have or things that will not be good for you in the long run. It may feel awful at the moment, and things you once delighted in may seem uninteresting to you now, but it's time to stop being melodramatic and to look around yourself carefully. You still have options and opportunities. Tap into the element of water, wash away your doldrums, and find solace and peace.

Keywords: Dissatisfaction, disappointment, moping, moodiness, melodrama. Wanting things you cannot have or that will not be beneficial in the long run. Allow the element of water to wash away your doldrums.

Reversed: Loss, remorse, minor depression, sadness.

Six of Cups

Two adorable blond children, a brother and sister, sit happily in the green grass and clover on a bright summer afternoon. They have arranged Sweet William flowers in six silver cups. Both of the children wear a watery shade of blue, and their clothes are practical and sturdy for playing outside. A pump bubbles out water to drink, should the children wish for it, and a quiet, shallow stream flows gently through the landscape. The little stream is deep enough to splash in and safe for the children to play by. Peaceful blue skies and a thatched cottage can be seen in the background. This is a simple time of tranquility, enchantment, and innocence. The siblings are creating happy memories while they play together. Life is uncomplicated, and children are very close to magick. Magick is never questioned by children… it simply *is*. In this card, imagination rules their world. The memories they are making are joyful and sweet. In the language of flowers, the Sweet William blossoms represent childhood and sweet memories.

Meanings

This card symbolizes happy memories from your childhood, old friends and family, and your past. It can indicate reunions—a surprise visit from a family member or classmate whom you may not have seen in years, a forgotten friend from your old stomping grounds, a former coven member who moved away, or a childhood sweetheart who may be making a return appearance in your life. The Six of Cups card may also be a notice that you need to adopt a more childlike type of wonder for the world around you. Let your imagination guide you into a new, creative project. Believe in magick again.

> **Keywords:** Happy memories, old friends, childhood, family and school reunions. Let your imagination soar. Believe in magick again.

> **Reversed:** Unhappy memories. Feeling sad over an ended relationship. Losing your joy in magick.

Seven of Cups

rranged on a bank of clouds are seven silver cups. Inside of each cup there is something wonderful, magickal, and different. A white-haired and bearded wizard with half-moon glasses is in the foreground. He wears flowing, watery blue robes with magickal symbols embroidered upon them. The wizard has on a tall, pointed hat, and he gestures with an open hand to you as if encouraging you to reach out and choose one of the seven silver cups. The wizard is offering you a choice. All of these choices are equally wonderful, and they all represent something different. One cup holds a tiny winged red dragon. The topmost cup has a small black kitten sitting inside of the cup. The third cup holds a tiny fairy-tale castle, and a fourth cup has a little rainbow shining out. A fifth cup holds jewels and gold coins, while a sixth cup has a tiny mermaid lounging inside. The seventh and final cup has a monarch butterfly emerging from it.

Meanings

Many wonderful choices lie before you. This is the card of precognitive dreams, symbols, and signs. Take a moment and choose one of the seven cups; now read along and see what it tells you about yourself. The red dragon represents the power of transformation and the element of fire; what sort of passion and power can you manifest in your world? The black kitten grants you the opportunity to work more closely with the animal kingdom and to find your own magickal familiar. The third cup's fairy-tale castle offers you the chance of stability, comfort, and the magick of hearth and home. The fourth cup shows you a rainbow—time to work on your communication skills and see what messages await you on Iris's magickal rainbow from the Temperance card. The fifth card holds jewels and gold coins, inviting you to dig in and work magick with the element of earth; focus on crystals, stones, minerals, and metals. The sixth card has a tiny mermaid who invites you deeper into the realm of the element of water; embrace your psychic gifts and emotions and see where they lead you. The final cup with the butterfly beckons you to the element of air. Sharpen your intellect, hone your instincts, and pay attention to your intuition. What sort of new knowledge will the element of air blow into your world?

> *Keywords:* Choice. Many wonderful options lie before you—choose one of these cups and their lessons for yourself.

> *Reversed:* Don't be fooled into making a decision for another; they will come to resent you for it. Indecisiveness, fantasy, illusion.

Eight of Cups

In the foreground are eight silver cups all stacked and balanced neatly in rows and sitting on the shoreline. Behind the eight cups, we see a young woman in a blue traveler's cloak with a sprig of blooming sweet peas tucked in her hair. The young woman is walking away from the cups, leaving them behind, and she is traveling at the water's edge. That she is walking in an in-between place is significant here. She is at the boundary of one realm and the next, namely the earth and sea. An unseen breeze blows/ruffles her cape a bit behind her. A crescent moon shines down from a nighttime sky where eight tiny stars twinkle. There are high cliffs in the distance, but the traveler keeps her eyes on the horizon. She has chosen to abandon things that are no longer necessary or are detrimental. As she travels down the beach, a dolphin spyhops out to see her. The dolphin was considered to be a messenger by the ancient Greeks. He appears in this card as if he is checking on the woman's progress. The young woman is moving on and moving forward. The blossoms in her hair are symbolic; in the language of flowers, pink sweet peas symbolize departure.

Meanings

This card symbolizes the need to move on in your life. The need to move forward might be a physical relocation such as moving for a job or moving to a new home, or this may be an emotional shift. Either way, the message of the Eight of Cups should be honored. If your move is emotional, then set some healthy boundaries. Put the past behind you and go forward with determination to a better, happier, and healthier place. If you are physically moving, then go forward and enjoy the positive changes in your life.

Keywords: Moving on with your life, leaving the past behind you, setting healthy boundaries.

Reversed: Abandoning success, risk of making a bad decision.

Nine silver cups are arranged in an arc across a covered banquet table. Behind the table, a pretty woman wearing a bright blue and green gown stands, smiling contentedly and pouring wine into one of the nine cups as if to welcome you to the feast. The hostess has mystical peacock feathers and a blue flower in her hair, and a necklace with nine stones around her throat. The tablecloth is pale aqua blue, and there are starfish and shells worked into the cloth's design for a visual link to the element of water. An arrangement of pineapples, grapes, apples, and a pumpkin are displayed artfully on the table as if a celebration is about to occur. The pineapple is a classic symbol of hospitality. The pumpkin, apples, and grapes speak of the bounty of the harvest season, and the pumpkin is associated with the moon and the element of water. In the background, a cauldron—a classic symbol of the Goddess—is simmering over a hearth fire.

Meanings

When the Nine of Cups turns up in a reading, expect that your social calendar will be filling up. This is the "hospitality" card. It also symbolizes welcome and confirms that you will be hosting an event or party for family and friends. If it appears in a reading with the Four of Wands, then expect to be very busy with social plans for the next few months. The Nine of Cups announces that you may find yourself hosting a sabbat or esbat celebration for your coven. This card can also represent community gatherings. Don't be surprised if you become involved in the organization and running of the sabbat celebration or community event. Enjoy the preparations and plans, and do not stress over them. Furthermore, this particular card is sometimes referred to as "the wish card." A wish is about to be granted.

Keywords: Hospitality, community, graciousness. Gatherings, festivals. A wish will be granted. Enjoyable celebrations with family, coven, and friends.

Reversed: Smugness, false pride. You are not as popular as you think you are. Unfriendliness.

Ten of Cups

A blond man and a brown-haired woman stand on the banks of a winding river. Arm in arm, they look up at the blue sky, where a vibrant rainbow shines above the family. Within the rainbow are ten silver cups. Each parent has one arm raised as if in celebration. While they embrace, their three young children happily dance, holding hands in a circle, beside them. The children add energy and excitement to this card. While the parents are celebrating quietly, the children, on the other hand, are spinning in a circle, their joy too much to contain. The children need to laugh, to move, and to dance through the flowers.

Pink verbena grows prettily in the surrounding meadow and at the family's feet. In the distance, green willow trees and a pretty cottage on a hill can be seen. The river in this card is a symbol of the happy emotions that flow through this scene. The pretty cottage on the hill is an obvious symbol of a joyful home. The willow tree is associated with goddess magick and the element of water. Finally, in the language of flowers, the pink verbena means a happy family bond.

Meanings

When the Ten of Cups shimmers into a reading, it is a positive omen. This is the card of the happy family and good marriage or stable relationship. This card also symbolizes the bond of friendship, the fellowship of community, or the emotional ties that form in a happy and close coven. Naturally, work and care are required to maintain these good relationships, but a positive and happy outcome will be achieved. Celebrate the loving relationships that you have in your life. Friends and family are precious; cherish them.

> **Keywords:** Love, imagination, fulfillment. Joy, good humor, happy family. Good home life, comfort and joy. Friendship, happy coven, being a part of the magickal community.

> **Reversed:** Dissatisfaction, not seeing the magick or the joy within your life. Feeling like an outsider in your family or coven. Being used as a scapegoat.

Page of Cups

The Page of Cups is shown here as a young teen on the brink of womanhood. The page is full of optimism and curiosity, and good humor lights up her hazel eyes. Her golden-brown hair is partially gathered back with a seashell headband, while her pale aqua dress and silver starfish earrings show her to be linked to the element of water. Around her throat is a necklace of simple sea glass. The Page of Cups holds a silver cup out before her in both hands. Inside the cup, a blue fish has appeared and is whispering secrets to her. The fish is inviting the page to look within to embrace the element of water and to explore her intuitive, magickal, and psychic talents. Behind the Page of Cups we see bright blue skies and the ocean. Surrounding the page a playful, sparkling wave with a crescent-moon shape is seen. This is another nod towards the feminine powers of the moon and its pull over the ocean tides and its power over us all. The page is not worried about the wave—she welcomes its playful splashing. After all, it's all part of the learning process. She is ready to dive in and begin her studies. The Page of Cup's adventures and the journey on her new magickal path have only just begun.

Meanings

When the Page of Cups splashes into a reading, you are being put on notice that new intuitive talents are about to emerge. Take this time to explore your gifts. Immerse yourself in the exploration of your intuition, empathy, clairvoyance, and other psychic talents. This court card may also symbolize a student just beginning their studies in the magickal arts. Embrace the fun of discovery, and put some joy back into your craft. As with all court cards, the page can represent an actual person. Typically, this will be a youth with blond or brown hair and blue, light hazel, or green eyes.

The message of the Page of Cups is to explore your magickal and psychic talents. Don't forget that magick is a joyous thing!

Keywords: Imagination. A student beginning magickal or psychic studies, discovering new psychic or magickal talents, embracing hope, and rediscovering the joy of your craft.

Associated Elements: Water and earth. Water is the suit of cups' related natural element, while all four pages are associated with the practical element of earth.

Reversed: Ignoring your intuition and psychic gifts. Refusing to commit to your magickal studies.

Knight of Cups

The handsome Knight of Cups is riding leisurely across a green field. A castle can be seen off in the distance, and clouds billow up in the background. Riding a beautiful gray horse, the knight follows a shimmering river towards that castle. The fair knight looks into a silver cup that he holds with a dreamy expression, as if he is seeing something reflected within. The cup held by the knight in this card can be thought of as the Grail, a traditional symbol of the Divine Feminine.

While the Knight of Cups has no sword showing, he still wears silver armor with a beautiful, flowing blue cape. This knight is elegant, not warlike. To further link him to the element of water, there is a wave motif on the trim of his horse's bridle. The two-tailed heraldic mermaids embroidered into the design of his cloak symbolize eloquence, loyalty, and truth. The mermaid is Melusine, an elemental spirit of springs and rivers. The Knight of Cups can be moody and passionate, but he always follows his heart. He is a symbol of courtly love and honor.

This knight could take you along on his quest—how do you think it will go? He may sweep you up into a romantic adventure or be your friend and ally accompanying you on a trip or a spiritual journey.

Meanings

A romantic and intuitive young man with blond hair and green or blue eyes will arrive soon. This court card often represents a sensitive, gallant, and chivalrous man. He is perceptive, empathic, and maybe a little reserved. He carefully protects his feelings, which is illustrated by the armor. The Knight of Cups characterizes someone who is faithful and true, who believes in magick, chivalry, and honor. They are the best friend a person could hope for, and they will probably love once and love deeply. This card often turns up when there is about to be a proposition or tryst. This card also symbolizes movement and travel or a kind or chivalrous act. Expect romance, visions of what is to come, magick, and new, creative opportunities.

The challenge of the Knight of Cups is this: will you scry within the surface of the cup to see what will be or look for a vision of your future lover? Flow with the element of water, and seek your mystical answer.

Keywords: A romantic young man. Romance, a proposition or a tryst. A chivalrous act, integration of the Divine Feminine, dreams, a quest, movement and travel.

Associated Elements: Water and fire. Water is the suit of cups' related natural element, while all four of the knights are associated with the energetic element of fire.

Astrological Association: Pisces.

Reversed: An unfaithful man. Vanity, deception. A womanizer, a sycophant.

The enchanting Queen of Cups sits on a shell and coral throne at the ocean's edge. A playful ocean breeze makes her platinum blond hair flutter back from her tranquil, beautiful face. The gentle waves in the background and gorgeous puffy clouds and blue skies set the tone for her calm and peaceful state of mind. The Queen of Cups is mystical and serene. She wears a pearl-encrusted silver crown with seven points on it, representing the seven seas. Her gown is a deep royal blue with a shell and water design and trimmed in pearls and silver. The queen holds the silver cup in both of her hands and is raising it up to eye level as if she is scrying upon the surface of the liquid within the cup.

A royal, rich necklace of sapphires, silver, and pearls is around the queen's throat. The pearls are linked to the element of water and prophetic dreams, and the silver is a receptive metal. The sapphires are naturally linked to the element of water, and their presence in the queen's silver crown and on her necklace strengthens her psychic awareness and is associated with love and serenity. A small bouquet of wood violets, white roses, and purple foxgloves lies in her lap. The flowers in her lap correspond to the element of water. The white roses symbolize loving emotions; the violets, faithfulness; and the foxgloves are a magickal flower of protection. The white roses scattered at her feet on the beach are left as an offering to the seas from whence she gathers her elemental power.

Meanings

This card represents a mature woman who is mystical, empathic, sensual, loving, and emotional. She is a water-sign woman, a loyal wife and mother, and a best friend. A natural Witch, she loves nature, animals, and her children and partner with equal intensity. This is a card that denotes a gifted psychic and a woman of strong intuitive and magickal talents. Physically this card may represent a fair woman with blond hair and blue or green eyes. This card has link to the High Priestess card as well, since both are cards of female power and intuition.

When the Queen of Cups washes up into your readings, remember that all psychic talents are affected by your emotions. The message of the Queen of Cups is reflection. Calm your emotions, and be loving and gentle. Allow the healing and magick of the element of water to wash over you and bring visions into your world.

Keywords: Serenity, love. A water-sign woman. Dedication, a loving wife and mother. A natural Witch or talented psychic. Reflection, emotional healing, the gifts of clairvoyance and empathy.

Associated Elements: Water and water. Water is the suit of cups' related natural element, while all four of the queens are also associated with the emotional element of water.

Astrological Association: Cancer.

Reversed: Vanity. Living in a fantasy land and ignoring the real world. Conceit, selfishness, a psychic vampire.

The King of Cups is seated on his throne beside the sea. To honor his element and the suit there are two-tailed mermaids and cups worked into the throne's design. This elemental king wears regal, intricate robes in shades of silver and royal blue, and he is cloaked in majestic purple. A heraldic bright aqua-blue mermaid is embroidered on the chest of his tunic, and silver waves decorate the hem of his robes. The mermaid represents eloquence, loyalty, and truth. The king's crown is made of gleaming silver, with sapphires and a stylized starfish. He also wears a jeweled livery collar, or chain of office, made of silver, blue sapphires, and pearls. The metals and the stones are all linked to the element of water. The silver is receptive. The blue sapphires enhance his psychic talents and his ability to be loving and fair. The lunar pearls exemplify the wonderful gems of the sea. Both of the king's arms rest on the arms of the throne, showing that he is relaxed and in control of his domain. In his right hand he holds a silver cup. In his left hand is a scepter topped with a shell; we also see that this is a married man, as he wears a wedding band on his left hand. The king looks straight ahead as if he is carefully considering both you and your request. The King of Cups is smiling kindly, and his blond hair, moustache, and beard have just a touch of gray in it, showing that he is older and wiser. In the background we can see the ocean and dolphins joyfully leaping out of the water.

Meanings

A mature, wise man who is well versed in the Craft. This card represents an individual who is artistic, intuitive, creative, and passionate. Physically he has dark blond to light brown hair with a touch of gray, and blue or green eyes. He is a good friend, a loving and attentive husband, and a devoted father. The King of Cups gives good, solid advice when asked. This card can represent a quiet man who keeps his emotions to himself but who can be moody. He is, however, deeply emotional, and he has a tough outer shell to disguise a very soft and loving interior. He often sees what most people would prefer to keep hidden. This card represents an individual who is an excellent mediator, psychically talented, and strong and fair.

The lesson from the King of Cups is that wisdom comes from looking within. Temper your counsel of others with compassion and affection.

Keywords: A water-sign man. A married, mature man well versed in the Craft. A loving husband and father, a good friend, a wise counselor. A creative personality. The gifts of intuition. Wisdom that comes from experience.

Associated Elements: Water and air. Water is the suit of cups' related natural element, while all four of the kings are associated with the wise and thoughtful element of air.

Astrological Association: Scorpio.

Reversed: Difficulty expressing emotions. Dishonesty, a domineering lover, a person taking unfair advantage over another who is less experienced.

Swords

Don't leave home without your sword—your intellect.
ALAN MOORE

The suit of swords symbolizes the element of air and all the magickal associations that float out from this element: wisdom, keen intellect, and truth. Swords cards point a clever way down a path to understanding through cutting-edge ideas, knowledge, discernment, and the powers of the mind. This suit illustrates the power of darker emotions, mental activity, intelligence, and prophecy. It develops the original spark of an idea through communication.

The elemental being associated with air is the faerie, so if you look closely at the swords cards, you will see a few winged faeries fluttering in them. Winged creatures such as hawks, falcons, songbirds, and dragonflies are also linked to the element of air and will make their appearance in this suit. There is also plant and flower magick incorporated in these card images. The flowers shown are either aligned to the element of air—such as lavender, mistletoe, and lily of the valley—or have specific messages from the language of flowers that are pertinent to the card.

In the swords suit, you will see intense landscapes. You will find high mountains, windswept places, moonlit boudoirs, midnight forests, and misty castles off in the distance.

The suit of swords is classically associated with people born under an airy zodiac sign: Gemini, Libra, and Aquarius. Physically the court cards of the swords suit represent people that have brown hair and gray, green, or hazel eyes. Furthermore, individuals who are drawn to the swords suit tend to be talkative, social, and well read. These intense and intelligent people let their thoughts and dreams lead the way. They are the clever planners and shrewd organizers of the world.

Ace of Swords

single silver sword hovers upright in mid-air and is the main focus of the card. Just behind the sword a lone red-tailed hawk flies through the air. A misty mountain range can be seen off in the background. The sky is blue with a hint of rosy, soft clouds, and dawn is just beginning to break. The Ace of Swords is associated with the element of air, as are mountains, windswept places, and raptors. The mountains depicted in the Ace of Swords show us that though we may face challenges, through endurance and perseverance we can triumph. The hawk in the Ace of Swords is a messenger. He invites us to move forward and to be open to new ideas and to discover our personal power and our true purpose in life. Success is obtainable; you need to reach out for it. This card illustrates that spiritual awareness leads us beyond fantasy to a real and lasting truth.

Meanings

The Ace of Swords is the most potent and pure form of the masculine element of air. When the Ace of Swords flies into your life, you are being put on notice that it is time to take action. This is a card of intellect, heroism, victory, justice, achievement, new beginnings, and winning battles. Another of this card's most important lessons is that now you have the chance for a new way of thinking. Cut through the fantasy and embrace what is. The truth hurts, but sometimes it can also heal and make room for a new, improved reality. Success is attainable; victory is near; go grab ahold of it with both hands!

Keywords: Success, truth, awareness, victory. Determination. Take action now. A clear perception leads to spirit and a closer connection to deity. The element of air.

Reversed: Illusion, confusion, cruelty, injustice. Get a grip on yourself, and work on finding balance.

woman with straight brown hair and bangs sits on a stone bench in front of a calm lake at twilight. Pretty mountains are seen in the distance. A crescent moon hangs low in the twilight sky. The woman is blindfolded and her arms are crossed over her chest; her hands are at her shoulders as if she is protecting her heart or closing herself off. She wears a flowing gown of ivory with sky-blue trim. While she is intense and on guard, she is no victim; she is keenly aware of her surroundings. By wearing a blindfold she is calmly relying on her other heightened senses to alert her to danger. Her sleeves are tightly fitted at the wrist, which keeps her hands free for handling the swords. She is ready to strike out if necessary. The woman is depicted at twilight because she is at an in-between state. Her back is to the moon and to the water to illustrate that she has turned away from her emotions, or at least shut them down for a time. Small clumps of the herb lavender grow on either side of the stone bench. In the language of flowers lavender symbolizes distrust, which is appropriate for this woman. Also, the herb lavender is associated with the element of air and is very protective when grown in a Witch's garden. Two faeries hover above the lavender, one on either side of the woman. Interestingly, the faeries face the water…perhaps they are helping to watch her back.

Meanings

When this card turns up in a reading, it is a warning that you have blocked off your heart and emotions and are holding in your feelings. You are literally refusing to see what is right in front of you. Your heart says one thing, while logic says another. The water in this card represents your emotions and the repression of them. Just as the woman has turned her back on her feelings, you need to be aware that you are blocked and have closed yourself off. You may think you have balance, but there is no resolution. Take a careful look at both sides of the situation. Consider your options: boundaries are a positive thing, but do not shut yourself off from others. Be like the water and the swords in this card—stay calm and reflect like the water while you work through this, and be balanced like the swords as you work for equilibrium and understanding.

Keywords: The heart and mind are not in agreement. Putting up unhealthy boundaries, holding in your true feelings, working for balance of heart and mind, considering your options.

Reversed: Being forced to face your suppressed emotions. Conflict, injustice, obstinacy.

Three of Swords

A large red heart is pierced by three swords. In the background a stormy sky and heavy rain clouds are seen. Three faeries hover about, looking dejected. A faerie couple embraces as if comforting each other, while the third faerie flies away. Blue ageratum flowers are falling from the rainy sky. While the heart is a symbol of love, truth, courage, and ethics, the three swords piercing the heart in this card sadly represent betrayal, heartbreak, and delay. The heavy, dark rain clouds symbolize the stormy emotions and tears that are present in your life at this time. In the language of flowers the blue ageratum means delay. This particular card illustrates the toughest times of heartbreak and the anguish of loss and betrayal.

Meanings

When the Three of Swords is dealt in a reading, it causes a visceral reaction. This is a brutally tough card; there is no polite or soft way to put it. When the Three of Swords turns up in a reading, it is like a sucker punch to the stomach. It hurts. This card, more than any other, illustrates the pain and loss that the querent is experiencing at this time. What you need to understand is that you will have to take the pain into your heart, accept it, shed your tears, and then move beyond it. Once you have accepted the pain and experienced the grief, then—and only then—can you move forward. This card may also stand for a delay to a project and plans or the painful karmic repercussions that are experienced when a manipulative spell backfires on the caster.

Keywords: Delay, personal betrayal, loss. A time of drama and tears. Sadness, conflict. A spell that has backfired.

Reversed: Destruction, strife. The healing process is blocked. Until you work through your grief, you will not be able to move on.

hazel-eyed woman in a yellow gown with purple trim stands to one side of the scene. A breeze ruffles the woman's long brown hair, and mountains can be seen in the background. The feather motif on the trim of her yellow gown indicates the element of air. To her right, three swords are displayed, neatly resting upon a castle wall. The woman looks a bit tired and holds the fourth sword point-down as if she is looking for a place to set it down. In her right hand she holds a few short branches of pussy willow. In the language of flowers the pussy willow symbolizes recovery from illness, and these are a reminder to rest and recover. The ivy growing on the castle walls has the magickal association of healing. Amethysts adorn the woman's elaborate headpiece, necklace, and belt. This enchanting purple stone promotes restful sleep, healing, and pleasant dreams. This card illustrates that while she is still taking care of herself and presenting her best face by wearing her lovely gown and beautiful jewels, the stress is starting to show. She craves some peace and solitude.

Meanings

When the Four of Swords is dealt in a reading, it is a sign that you need to take some personal downtime—a retreat or a day off so you can recoup lost energy and find your strength again. The querent may be feeling overwhelmed by demands and stress. They may feel the need to get away and to withdraw from the hectic and daily grind of life. This card symbolizes that you need to allow yourself time to recover from an illness. It may also represent a need to step away from group magick for a bit. You may need to practice solitarily for a time. You will find the solutions to your magickal problems quietly and on your own.

> *Keywords:* Taking some downtime for yourself. Resting and allowing yourself to fully recover from an illness. Recouping lost energy. Working magick as a solitary for a while, and finding your focus.

> *Reversed:* Feeling that you have been banished from a group. Rejection, exhaustion.

Five swords are fanned out across a beautiful bright blue sky. Pearly white clouds are illuminated, and just beneath the gathered points of the five swords is a gorgeous iridescent dragonfly, a symbol for the element of air, the Faery realm, and illusion. Five faeries fly merrily around the swords, uncaring of their sharp edges and any possible danger. But what do you suppose is the most dangerous aspect of this card, the sharp edges of the swords or the possible trickery of the fae? This card shows that your pride was hurt, but it's not fatal; do not overreact. You may feel embarrassed at the moment, but most of what you are so humiliated about is an illusion. The dragonfly represents a need to gain a new perspective and to make a change. The faeries encourage you to learn to laugh at yourself a bit, to see through others' trickery, and to keep moving forward.

Meanings

When the Five of Swords appears in a reading, it is a signal that the querent is feeling humiliated and embarrassed. This is only a partial defeat, and they are still in control. Don't give up! Shift things around and look for more possibilities. Allow the element of air to bring some fresh air and a new perspective into your life. Heed the message of the dragonfly and see through the illusions of others. Transform your life into something bright and wonderful.

Keywords: Embarrassment, illusion, trickery. Learn to laugh at yourself and keep going forward.

Reversed: Humiliation, carrying a grudge, conflict with a domineering person.

young man sits in the back of a small wooden boat. His muscular arms are bare. He wears a soft purple vest and gray pants as he paddles his way across the water towards a distant shore. In the distance, surrounding the lake, you can see mountains. A breeze blows his brown hair back from his face, and we can see just a bit of his right profile—the man is content and concentrating upon his journey. To link this card further to the element of air, there is a dragonfly motif along the sides of the yellow boat. Inside the wooden boat are six swords standing up, point down, and arranged neatly in front of him. The swords are not damaging the boat; perhaps they are plugging up the holes. These swords represent that even though you carry your troubles and concerns with you, you do not have to be weighed down by them. The blue skies and clear horizon indicate that this is a good time for travel.

Meanings

Traditionally, when the Six of Swords sails into a reading, it means travel over water. Today, it shows movement and progress of any kind. The querent may be planning a trip for pleasure or business. This card signifies that it is a good time for movement, change, and the experience that travel brings. Expect forward movement, improvement to the current situation, a new job, moving to a new home, and, of course, travel for pleasure. Enjoy the journey; there is smooth sailing ahead.

Keywords: Travel over water. Movement, a new job. Moving to a new home. Travel for pleasure. Progress, improvement, and smooth sailing ahead.

Reversed: Short-term improvement. Challenges to your progress. Travel delays or complications.

man carts off five swords with a satisfied smirk on his face. He is leaving two more swords behind but is very pleased with what loot he has managed to obtain. The man's tunic is golden yellow, with an airy feather motif at the bottom. Around his neck an upright pentacle pendant is seen. He looks pleased with himself and the five swords he carries, and he is on the verge of laughing. He has used his street smarts, confidence, and intelligence to take his prize and avoid any opposition. In the background we see that storm clouds are blowing past and there are colorful and festive tents, perhaps from a fair, in the background. The banners from these tents are flapping in a breeze as the storm and the wily man leave the area. All of the skills associated with the element of air and the suit of swords, such as intelligence, cunning, and foresight, are illustrated in this card.

Meanings

When the Seven of Swords card blows into a reading, it is a nudge to come up with some new schemes and/or tactics. It's time to be clever and creative. This card denotes a smart, resourceful person, one who avoids or evades confrontation. By doing so, he shrewdly takes the wind out of his opponent's sails. Look at things from a new perspective. Come up with a new solution to the same old problems. Think outside the box and you will experience a victory and a breakthough.

Keywords: New schemes, new solutions. Thinking outside the box. Relying on your street smarts. Partial victory, evasion, cunning, foresight.

Reversed: Allowing fear to hold you back. Not seizing opportunities. Timid behavior.

Eight of Swords

woman in a mauve gown is bound and blindfolded. A breeze blows her brown hair and the tails of the blindfold off to the side and away from her face. Around her, eight swords are stuck in the grass at various points in a loose circle. In the background we see a river and the outlines of a castle in the mist. The river illustrates the emotions streaming through the scene, while the mist-shrouded castle represents goals that may seem hard to realize. Around the swords and in the grass grows blooming nightshade. In the enchanting language of flowers the nightshade symbolizes false, dark thoughts. The woman in this card could ease her way through and out of the circle of swords—she does have options—but fear has taken over. She seems frozen, and her false, dark thoughts, or her overactive imagination, has made things seem worse than they truly are. The skies above her show that the sun is rising, and a rosy dawn light is breaking through and beginning to burn off the mist. She should pull off that blindfold, step beyond any perceived restrictions, and turn and face the new day.

Meanings

When this card turns up in a reading, it speaks of restriction and of feeling trapped and sad at the moment. However, if the individual would stop overreacting and feeling sorry for themselves and would pull off that emotional blinder, they would see a way out. Things are not as bad as they may appear. Happiness is possible, the sun is breaking through, and new opportunities can emerge. This card may also represent a Witch who is fearful of ritual or of their own initiation. Think of the classic challenge given to most blindfolded initiates: "It is better to rush upon this blade than to enter the circle with fear in your heart. How do you enter?" They have to answer without fear or they are denied entrance into the coven. What can you learn from this card? Look again at the description and symbolism, and find your answers. Fear has no place in the Craft.

Keywords: Restriction, feeling trapped. Overreacting to the situation. Things are not as bad as they seem; you can work your way out of this. Fear of initiation or ritual.

Reversed: Feeling completely helpless, overwhelmed. Mild situational depression. Leaving a coven out of fear of the unknown.

Nine of Swords

woman wearing a nightgown lies dramatically in her boudoir at night. She has the back of her hand on her forehead, in a swoon from being either emotionally or physically drained. She is clearly overwhelmed, and her other hand trails limply to the floor. Her long hair flows back across the pillows and reveals a bite mark on her neck—two puncture wounds as if from a vampire. The waning moon illuminates the gothic window, while nine swords are arranged on the wall, cagelike and blocking the view out of the window. The yellow primrose flowers embroidered on the bed linens symbolize sorrow. The woman may be reaching up towards the handle of the bottom sword...perhaps she is finally ready to defend herself, to break free and to stop the drama. Or maybe she needs to feel sorry for herself just a bit longer.

Meanings

This is the "drama queen" card. When it turns up in a reading, it symbolizes a person who is always having a crisis or causing drama in coven dynamics or social situations. They may be an emotional or psychic vampire, or they themselves could be the willing victim of such an attack. As this is a nine of the suit, it also symbolizes that you are near the end of the problem. Things have reached their peak and should begin to settle down—as long as you do not give way to dramatics. Decide to pick up the sword, to be proactive, and to defend yourself and your personal energies. Furthermore, this card can represent the karmic repercussions of poor judgment or backlash from a manipulative magickal act. I think of this card as a perfect illustration of baneful magick that has returned to its sender times three.

> *Keywords:* "Drama queen" card. Psychic or emotional vampire or victim. Baneful magick returned to its sender times three.

> *Reversed:* Suspicion, fear, anxiety. Morbid fantasy, cruel behavior. Uninvited, unrepentant psychic vampire.

A man's body lies facedown in the grass. There are ten swords stabbing him in the back. He has brown hair, and his cloak is gray. Behind him the sun is setting, and in a tree's gnarled and twisted branches an owl with bright yellow eyes sits and watches over the body. The owl, also a creature of the element of air, is a classic symbol of magick, mystery, and inner wisdom. The landscape in the background is ominous, dark, and threatening. There are so many swords in the man that it must have taken a group of people to do this. The lack of blood in the card reminds us that this is symbolic act and not a literal one. The man portrayed here trusted when he shouldn't have or ignored his own instincts, and now he has paid the price by being betrayed many times over. A lone plant of purple blooming monkshood grows near the body. In the language of flowers monkshood warns that a deadly foe is near. Clearly this man did not pay attention to the poisonous herb's warning.

Meanings

When the Ten of Swords rolls into a reading, you have to ask yourself, "Why did you not listen to your own instincts?" This card is a vivid illustration of being stabbed in the back. This shows betrayal from a loved one, friend, or coven member. This what happens when you ignore your inner voice and gut hunches that something is wrong. By ignoring the warning signs and not paying heed to your own instincts that trouble was brewing, you have paid the price. This card can also symbolize being involved with a toxic group of people, such as in a job environment or even in a coven where you are not cherished but instead made to feel like an outsider. If your instincts are warning you that you don't belong, then you need to be wise, like the owl, and fly away from the group and all of their negativity.

> **Keywords:** A coven where you do not feel accepted or cherished. A toxic group of people. Betrayal, being stabbed in the back, ignoring your instincts.

> **Reversed:** Physical harm from another. A negative or immoral group of people. Unfairly becoming the scapegoat for a family or coven and all of its problems.

Page of Swords

tall, thin teenage boy stands on a green plain. A strong breeze is blowing his metal hawk pendant that he wears as a talisman around his neck. In both hands the Page of Swords easily holds a sword aloft. He is checking himself for the moment and is intensely reviewing the situation. Will he strike out and defend himself or will he put the sword down? It could go either way, as he appears to be putting you on notice and psyching himself up for a possible battle all at the same time. His shirt is a soft, cloudy gray color, with yellow trim and pale blue hawks embroidered on the sleeves. This traditional heraldry symbolizes that he is impatient and will not stop until his goals are reached. Behind him are blue skies and white, fluffy, fair-weather clouds. Off in the far distance, at the horizon, mountains can be seen. In this court card the element of air is paired with the intensity and quick, moody reactions of a young man. It is anybody's guess as to whether he will rein in his temper and react appropriately.

Meanings

When this card lands in a reading, it means that you need to think quickly and act decisively but keep your temper in check. You need to remain vigilant and to be on guard for trouble or conflict, but you should use your wit and not brute force. You do have the ability to quickly put an end to nonsense and petty arguments with either quick actions or a few well-chosen words. This card may physically represent an intense, impulsive, and active young person with brown hair and green or hazel eyes. The hawk symbolizes messages, and when it appears in your life it is always a sign from deity to pay attention to what is going on around you.

The message of the Page of Swords is that caution, cleverness, and tact are needed at this time. Try for tact before you take a swipe at your opponent.

Keywords: Vigilance, caution. Standing on guard for trouble or conflict. Putting an end to petty conflicts with a few well-chosen words. An intense and intelligent young man.

Associated Elements: Air and earth. Air is the suit of swords' related natural element, while all four of the pages are associated with the practical element of earth.

Reversed: Tension, rash actions. Using physical force when it is unnecessary.

The handsome young Knight of Swords and his war horse are leaping into battle. In the knight's right hand he holds up a sword as he charges confidently into the fray. With his left hand he holds lightly on to the reins of his powerful Friesian horse. He is in control and at his best. The Knight of Swords is a dangerous, magnificent, and daring warrior. His visor is up on his helmet, allowing him to see what is coming without impediment. His bright yellow cloak streams behind him, and his well-used armor is dark silver with hints of blue. The knight's cloak and his horse's bridle and trim are yellow and detailed with a heraldic hawk design, which symbolize eagerness and the thrill of the chase. The colors and heraldry clearly illustrate the knight's link to the element of air. In the background behind the knight and the horse we see storm clouds rolling in over the plains. The Knight of Swords is all about valor, momentum, shrewdness, bravery, and service. The element of air pushes along the perception of speed; the knight's strength and forward motion are evident. He is a fearless individual, and his ideals and beliefs propel him forward. He stands up for what he believes in. This knight illustrates the very best qualities of the suit of swords: balance, energy, intelligence, and drive, coupled with responsibility.

Meanings

If we had to sum up this court card in two words, they would be "no fear." When this card comes roaring into a reading, expect excitement, movement, and adventure. There is a need for action, and it is time for you to dive in and be the hero. This court card represents a passionate and exciting young man with brown hair and gray or hazel eyes. This is an individual who is clever and capable in a crisis. He is shrewd and dynamic, and possesses a razor-sharp wit. He may be a bit arrogant, but it is all a part of his charm. This is the card of the soldier and the warrior. The Knight of Swords will roar into your life bringing exploration, communication, new ideas, and change.

The challenge from the Knight of Swords is to stand up for yourself and your beliefs. Rapid movement and transformation is blowing your way—hang on and enjoy the ride.

> *Keywords:* No fear. Courage, momentum. Swift change and progress. A clever, brave, and capable man. Stand up and defend your position.

> *Associated Elements:* Air and fire. Air is the suit of swords' related natural element, while all four of the knights are associated with the energetic element of fire.

> *Astrological Association:* Gemini.

> *Reversed:* Conflict, misplaced aggression, no progress.

Queen of Swords

The beautiful Queen of Swords sits at the top of a high mountain, and bright white clouds are billowing in the wind. Her throne is sturdy but elegant, with carved songbirds worked into the armrests and the overall design. The wind swirls her long brown hair around and behind her thoughtful face. She has smoky gray eyes and a serious expression, as if she is plotting something or considering her best options. In her right hand the queen holds up a beautiful, gleaming sword. With her left hand she seems to be beckoning to someone. The queen wears a white gown accented with azure. A sky-blue cloak with white feather trim flows over her shoulders and back. Her crown has sharp, dramatic spikes and is set with yellow topaz stones. The yellow topaz in her crown encourages a successful attainment of personal goals. She wears a large necklace of blue topaz around her throat. The blue topaz gem evokes truth and wisdom.

In her lap is a small bouquet of fragrant herbs that are associated with the element of air. She holds lavender, which is protective, and lily of the valley, which in the language of flowers means a return to happiness. A blue jay sits on the back of her throne, and another is on the ground next to her. The blue jays remind us to call upon our own sense of sovereignty—to develop our own talents, be fearless, and walk our talk with integrity, just as the Queen of Swords does. The winged faerie that hovers nearby is a sylph, an elemental creature of the air, and seems to be attending the queen.

Meanings

The Queen of Swords is a brown-haired woman with fair to hazel eyes. She is clever and ingenious, with a dry wit and razor tongue. When this card breezes into a reading, it can herald a time when you need to pay attention to your own instincts and intuition. New ideas are blowing in; it may be time to try something new. This card classically represents an air-sign woman—a woman who is career oriented, honest, focused, and successful in whatever she sets out to do. She may be sarcastic at times, but she is smart, blunt, and determined. She will rule her home and family with the same ruthless organization she applies to her career. Her communication skills are top notch; she may be a scholar, a writer, or a speaker. Though men are attracted to her for her looks, they tend to back off when they discover how smart and honest this queen is. She has no time for falsehood or ignorance. The Queen of Swords may represent a woman who is slow to trust others, especially in relationships, and a woman who may prefer to stand on her own. This queen will listen to her head first and logically consider her options before she trusts her heart.

The message from the Queen of Swords is this: assert your independence, stand up for yourself, follow your intuition, and try something new.

Keywords: An air-sign woman. Wisdom, independence, intuition, assertiveness. Personal development. Walk your talk.

Associated Elements: Air and water. Air is the suit of swords' related natural element, while all four of the queens are associated with the emotional element of water.

Astrological Association: Libra.

Reversed: A woman who has closed off her feelings and established very high boundaries. Isolation, gossip. A vindictive woman.

King of Swords

The King of Swords is a handsome middle-aged man with brown hair, moustache, and beard. His eyes are dark and attentive, and he has a serious and thoughtful expression, as if he is carefully considering the matter before him. The king sits on a throne that is carved with hawks in an interwoven design. Behind the throne we can see green trees, a blue sky, and windswept mountains. The King of Swords wears a spiky golden crown of knowledge with magickal blue topaz stones in it. Topaz stones bring truth and forgiveness and help to illuminate your path. His armor is elegant and well used, as is befitting for a king. This king announces his associations to the element of air with a yellow tunic and golden cape trimmed in feathers. In his right hand he holds up the sword of truth, and sunlight gleams off the sword. He sits at attention on his throne and looks as if he will move forward quickly and decisively if action is called for. In his other gloved hand he holds a hooded peregrine falcon. The falcon that sits lightly on his hand is calmly waiting for the moment to go hunting. The falcon symbolizes swiftness, accuracy, and cunning, and it encourages us to be ready to act at the most opportune time for the greatest success.

Meanings

The King of Swords is an authority figure. When this card soars into a reading, you need to be aware that your actions may be called into question. This is the card for rulers, leaders, and the wielders of justice. The King of Swords has links to the Emperor and the Justice cards, as the King of Swords concerns himself with matters of right and wrong, and also personal integrity and honor. This card quietly calls into question the wisdom of your personal choices, and he also announces that it is time to turn your knowledge into action. This man sees the world in black or white; there are no shades of gray for him. He is successful, clever, reserved, and a tad intellectual. He has a good head for business and may be a member of the armed forces, a security guard, a detective, or a police officer. The King of Swords also represents a mature man with brown hair and dark eyes who values his integrity above all else. He relies heavily on his common sense and believes in only what can be proven. Like the best kings of old, he is a wise and fair leader who sits in judgment because he must and who is ready to defend his kingdom should the situation deem it necessary.

The lesson of the King of Swords is to turn your knowledge into action while remaining fair and just.

Keywords: An air-sign man. Authority, a fair leader, judgment. Justice, reason, logic, truth. Ethics, honor, swiftly turning knowledge into action.

Associated Elements: Air and air. Air is the suit of swords' related natural element, while all four of the kings are also associated with the wise and thoughtful element of air.

Astrological Association: Aquarius.

Reversed: A judgmental, arrogant person. A domineering, unkind man. A dangerous individual.

Wands

Wands signify the desire for growth,
the inspiration that moves things,
the desire that leads the way ...

Mary K. Greer

This deck is based on the Rider-Waite-Smith system, which aligns the wands suit with fire and the swords suit with air. The suit of wands symbolizes the element of fire and all the magickal associations that radiate from this element. Wands are all about enthusiasm, confidence, and ambition. In the Witches Tarot the wand itself is a blooming branch of hawthorn adorned with red ribbons. The hawthorn tree is a magickal tree that is associated with the element of fire, which is why I chose it for this suit. Hawthorn blossoms are used in protection and fertility spells.

The hawthorn, sometimes referred to as "thorn," is part of the magickal trinity of faerie trees. The oak, ash, and thorn (or hawthorn) make up that triad. In the language of flowers the fragrant hawthorn blossom symbolizes hope. Wands cards illuminate a path to understanding through physical action, movement, and optimism. They illustrate the power of adventure, passion, and excitement. The wands suit explores the desire to create. Finally, this suit often is associated with career and business. The suit of wands corresponds to people born under a fiery zodiac sign: Aries, Leo, and Sagittarius. Physically the court cards of the wands suit represent people who have very fair complexions, with either pale blond or red hair and light blue or green eyes.

Individuals who are drawn to the wands suit tend to be athletic, enthusiastic, charismatic, and outgoing; they let their actions lead the way. They are the go-getters and the movers and shakers of this world.

awn is breaking, and we see a blooming hawthorn branch stuck firmly into the grassy hill. The wand is a bit reminiscent of a Maypole, with its crisscrossed ribbons and a fire-red streamer blowing in the breeze. According to tradition, the hawthorn tree was a popular choice for Maypoles. Behind the wand there are green rolling hills and a turreted castle on a hill. The castle in the background represents the reward that waits for you after your quest for knowledge and advancement is completed. The hawthorn is associated with the element of fire, making it fitting as the wand representation in this tarot for Witches. The hawthorn flowers flourishing on the single wand symbolize ideas that emerge and then blossom from our minds. In the language of flowers the hawthorn blossom symbolizes hope. A bright red butterfly flutters to the side of the wand. The butterfly symbolizes transformation, regeneration, and joy. It is going to be a beautiful day and one full of promise.

Meanings

The Ace of Wands is the most potent and pure form of the masculine element of fire. This card shows the creative fire, or energy, that cannot be contained and now is bursting forth in bloom. The Ace of Wands helps to reveal the creative path or the career path that you are on. Your hard work is turning your ideas into a successful reality. This is an auspicious card if the querent is considering a new job or is up for a promotion at work. The Ace of Wands symbolizes power, new beginnings, a birth, success, a new home, a promotion or a new job, ambition, passion, enthusiasm, and growth.

Keywords: Creativity, courage, optimism. Ambition, career and business, positive starts, a birth, transformation, or even a new home. Your hard work is turning ideas into a successful reality. The element of fire.

Reversed: Disappointment. Not being able to see the happiness that is right in front of your face. Lack of direction and focus. Wasted energy and magickal talents.

An auburn-haired man stands looking out over the water at sunset. The man is wealthy and successful, wearing a fur-trimmed, gold-colored coat and a burgundy-colored cape. He is before a waist-high stone wall. In the man's left hand he holds a tall blooming hawthorn wand. To the man's right a second wand is standing upright against the stone wall. The man appears to be holding the world in the palm of his right hand, yet he continues to gaze out off into the distance as if he is looking for more. Is he feeling walled in by his choices? Off in the distance we see two ships on the water and mountains at the horizon. The ships on the water symbolize the man's hopes and dreams of the future. The man is preparing for a favorable change. On the edge of the stone wall, a calico cat sits contentedly next to the man as if to watch over those ships with him. Calico cats are considered to be lucky, and their three colors are said to represent the Triple Goddess. The calico cat is his ally and friend and is a symbol of mentoring, support, and friendly advice that will help to guide him to success.

Meanings

This card represents partial success. While others may think you hold the world in the palm of your hand, you may still feel like you are unsure of where to go next. Such scenarios occur when an unexpected promotion or career advancement leaves you feeling unsure of what to do next. There is a partial success, and you may feel like you are at the halfway point of your personal goals. There are choices and serious decisions to be made. But look around you—there is help, support, and advice from a mentor. Take their good advice, and enjoy this new business or career opportunity. Finally, this card can symbolize a successful business partnership.

> *Keywords:* Preparation for a favorable change. Partial
> success. Good advice from a mentor. Successful
> business partnerships.

> *Reversed:* Possible delays, unfulfilled promises.
> Indecision, disillusionment.

brown-haired young man stands high on a cliff over-
looking the water and the horizon. His high vantage
point allows him to see the big picture. In his left hand
he holds up a blooming and beribboned wand of hawthorn. Just
behind him two more tall wands are planted in the ground as
if in support. The man has a band around his head to keep his
hair out of his eyes and his vision of the future clear. He wears
an orange tunic and a rich red cloak; these fiery colors are a
visual link to the element of fire, which correlates with the suit
of wands. The young man gazes out on the calm sea, where
there are two ships sailing in the distance, as if he is waiting
for his ships to come in. Perhaps he is waiting to board one of
those boats and set off on new adventures so he can explore the
unknown. He is actively watching, waiting, and letting events
unfold. This is an exciting card and one full of possibilities and
impending success. The bright sky and calm seas illustrated in
this card show that this is an optimistic card and that the future
looks bright.

Meanings

When the Three of Wands turns up in a reading, it illustrates
a time of expectation. The querent may be waiting for news
about a project or proposal. The overall theme of this card is
optimism and active waiting. It shows the beginning of a project and the hope that comes from making plans for a new career
or life. Remember that things are always in motion—nothing
is at rest, and change is constant. The Three of Wands usually
represents the person receiving the reading. This card may also

be nudging you towards taking on more of a leadership role at work or in your coven. This is a time of expansion and growth. Be like the watcher in the Three of Wands: keep a sharp eye, and allow events to unfold. There is reason to be optimistic and to have hope—the future looks bright.

> *Keywords:* Active waiting. Everything is in constant motion. Expansion, growth. Taking on a leadership role. Keeping an eye on your future goals. The future looks bright.

> *Reversed:* Unrealistic expectations. Disagreement with coworkers. Conflicting spiritual views with coven-mates.

Four large and tall blooming hawthorn wands are posted into green grass, creating a large square. Long red ribbons from the wands flutter in the breeze. A lush and beautiful garland of flowers is draped between the four wands, creating a bower of sorts. Four women, one to represent each of the natural elements, are dancing beneath the bower. Each woman holds a bouquet of flowers. The woman who represents fire has red hair and a flame-colored gown. She holds a bouquet of red roses, symbolizing passion and energy. The second dancer, who signifies the element of water, has blond hair and is wearing a royal-blue gown. She holds a bouquet of white roses, symbolizing loving emotions. The third lady, representing the element of air, has dark brown hair, wears a saffron-colored gown, and clutches a posy of yellow roses. Her sunshine roses stand for friendship and happiness. The fourth woman has golden-brown hair and is wearing a green gown, representing the element of earth. She holds a simple bouquet of greenery and daisies, which signify growth and affection. All of the flowers in the garland above the elemental dancers correspond to the element of fire. The sunflower is for fame and success, the marigold symbolizes affection and the sun, and red carnations bring fascination, healing, and love. In the background the sky is a sunny yellow at dawn, and a castle can be seen. The castle represents security and goals that are achieved. A white and orange cat sits seriously in the foreground, like a sentinel, at the base of one of the wands. Cats are linked to the element of fire, and this little feline seems to be watching over the proceedings.

Meanings

When the Four of Wands dances into a reading, get ready to party! This card symbolizes celebrations such as birthday parties and, of course, baby and bridal showers. This may be a celebration with a family or a coven. This is the celebration of a happy event, a graduation, an anniversary, or a lavish and fun sabbat observance. The Four of Wands classically is interpreted as a fertility card, which links it to the sabbat of Beltane. This card announces an opportunity and a time to share joy with another. It may also represent a time of creativity and freedom of expression.

Keywords: Celebration, rejoicing over a happy event. Freedom, parties, baby and bridal showers, sabbat celebrations. Fertility, creativity, freedom of expression.

Reversed: Even when this card is reversed, it still maintains its positive message, only now the celebration is a big surprise. Now that you know, try to act surprised anyway!

Five of Wands

Five magnificent dragons are being flown into battle through the clouds. Each of the dragon's riders carry a blooming wand of hawthorn. One dragon is purple, to represent spirit; there is a blue dragon for water, a solid green dragon for earth, a gold and green dragon for air, and a bright red dragon to represent the element of fire. The riders' vastly different appearances offer a clue to this card's true meaning. Some of these riders are in armor and seem very intense, with aggressive postures, while two others seem to be more leisurely flying in, as if to see what all the ruckus is about. This is a personality clash and a skirmish. Dragons have a reputation for being fierce and ferocious but also wise and magickal all at the same time. Besides the usual elemental association of fire, the five dragons are also linked to each of the four natural elements, including a fifth element, that of spirit.

Meanings

When the Five of Wands soars into your reading, it shows that minor annoyances and petty arguments need to be dealt with. There are different opinions all wanting to be heard. This card symbolizes bickering between coven mates, friends, or coworkers. This card tells you that challenges are ahead and that you will need to be very clear in communicating your goals and desires to another. There may be petty troubles at your job or a little healthy competition. Put your game face on and put some effort into your problem solving, and you will see positive results.

Keywords: Competition, conflict, disagreements, challenges. Petty squabbling at work or within the coven. Put some effort into your problem solving to see positive results.

Reversed: Rivalry, disruption to your plans. Serious personality clashes or jealousy within your coven. Severe conflict at your place of employment. Power plays.

proud warrior returns triumphantly from battle. Five other wands can be seen being held up behind the rider and in the background as if by a crowd as he moves past them. In the background the sky is blue and a bright sun shines down on the rider and horse. The warrior is tired but looks pleased to be home. He wears golden armor, denoting his status, and a fire-red tunic with gold knotwork featuring dragons, the elemental creature of fire. The dragons symbolized on the warrior's tunic are interwoven upon themselves and represent the never-ending cycle of nature and life. The man's red, flowing cape has gold knotwork in the trim and trails over the back of his brown horse. The horse's parade cloak is also a bright red, with a matching dragon knot motif. These vibrant, fiery colors on the warrior's armor, tunic, and cloak indicate pride and accomplishment. The soldier holds in his right hand a tall blooming hawthorn wand; tied to that wand with a red ribbon is a green laurel wreath, which illustrates his triumphant return. Classically a laurel wreath symbolizes the God's favor. In the language of flowers the laurel leaf declares achievement. Dragons, naturally, are associated with the element of fire. In our fire-associated wands suit, the dragon represented in this card is symbolic. Dragons were popular in heraldic designs, as they represent courage, leadership, and overcoming obstacles.

Meanings

This is a victory card symbolizing achievement, recognition, compliments, success, accomplishment, and well-deserved accolades after hard work. You can overcome any obstacle if you work at it. This card can also remind us to hang in there. Times may be tough, but you will get through it and come out victorious if you keep trying.

Keywords: Victory, achievement. Recognition for a job well done. Compliments and success. Accomplishment after hard work.

Reversed: Delay in a project. Delay to your success. Not being recognized for your hard work. A crossed condition.

fit and trim young man holds a blooming hawthorn wand out horizontally in front of his chest. Behind him are cliffs in the background that represent the unknown, but the sky is brightening up and the clouds have parted, which is a visual clue that all is well here. The young man is taking a stand and is wearing flame colors of golden yellow, orange, and red to help visually link him to the element of fire. He charges towards the other wands confidently, as if he is enjoying the challenge. He is independent, clever, and more than capable of handling whatever life throws at him. This card symbolizes adrenalin, enthusiasm, and ambition. The young man in this card not only has the will to succeed, he relishes the chance to put his mental, physical, and magickal skills to the test.

Meanings

When the Seven of Wands turns up in a reading, it is a notice that you are about to face a challenge—one you will thoroughly enjoy. It may be a sort of personal test, where you take on the challenge just for the fun of it and to see just how far you can advance your skills, be they magickal or mundane. This card shows the use of muscle and movement with restraint and style. Your enthusiasm, ambition, and wit will serve you well here. This card appearing in a reading assures that you will overcome obstacles and rise above them with style, wit, and humor.

Keywords: Adrenaline, enthusiasm, ambition. A challenge. Putting your skills to the test. Overcoming magickal or mundane obstacles with style, wit, and humor.

Reversed: Lack of confidence, anxiety, indecision.

Eight of Wands

*E*ight blooming hawthorn wands adorned with red ribbons shoot down from a beautiful blue sky. In the background we see a silver lake, green valley, and mountains. The tranquil backdrop is in direct contrast to the eight wands that are rushing into view. The eight wands are coming back to earth, as it were. This can symbolize that many creative possibilities are falling into place. Also, the journey is coming to the happy end; all you hoped for is about to occur, and success is at hand. Excitement, activity, change, and movement are the messages of this card. The Eight of Wands is one of the few Minor Arcana cards that does not have any people, animals, or creatures in it; all we see is landscape and the eight wands hurtling towards the ground. This card is basic and simple in the best possible way, and so is its meaning. This is a card of movement and manifestation.

Meanings

When the Eight of Wands flies into a reading, it is a notice that projects that were once delayed are coming to a swift completion. This is a positive and exciting card full of motion and action. Spells that were cast will happily manifest now. Often this card will symbolize travel for business or pleasure, and typically this is travel by air. The Eight of Wands can also mean long-distance communication between business partners. This is the time where fresh ideas and creativity rule, and swift and decisive action is the order of the day.

Keywords: Movement, action. Things coming to a swift completion. The positive manifestation of spellwork. Travel for business or pleasure and typically travel by air. Long-distance communication.

Reversed: A situation that drags on forever. Spells that stall. Trouble with air travel. Cancelled flights.

strong and determined-looking woman is dressed in red with a large heraldic dragon embroidered upon the center of her tunic. She wears a silver pentagram amulet for protection around her throat. The woman has deep wine-red hair and holds one blooming hawthorn wand easily and diagonally across her body like a quarterstaff. Both a Witch and a warrior, she has on sturdy brown pants and leather boots as she stands at the ready to defend her turf. Eight other wands are posted into the green grass and arranged behind her as if they are creating a barrier. In the background the sun is setting beautifully over the mountains and casting long shadows across the grass and the flowers. The setting sun symbolizes that the warrior's test is soon coming to a successful end, and that her diligence has paid off. In the grass at the base of the wands, St. John's wort is blooming in places. The herb St. John's wort is associated with fire and the Midsummer sabbat, and it also symbolizes physical and magickal protection.

Meanings

When the Nine of Wands turns up in a reading, it is a notice to be on guard against trouble, mischief, gossip, and baneful magicks. Now is the time to be alert to trouble and be vigilant with protecting yourself and your professional or magickal reputation. You may need to defend yourself, so be alert and stay on guard. Stamina, courage, and conviction is needed at this time. Magickal protection work may be required. You may not feel like you have the fortitude for any more dramas, but stand firm and be strong. Defend your turf and your reputation skillfully and vigorously. The suit of wands is all about creativity and ambition; you can do this. Draw some boundaries, call upon your inner resources, and stand strong.

> *Keywords:* Stamina, courage, protection. Be alert to trouble. Protect yourself and your reputation. Stand strong, be on guard. Magickal protection work may be required.

> *Reversed:* Paranoia, fear of failure, lack of courage. You look to others for a rescue when you should look to yourself first.

An old man is traveling away from us and down a dirt path towards a castle. He is carrying a bundle of ten blooming hawthorn wands over his left shoulder. The old man is slightly hunched over, as if his burden is just a tad too heavy for him to manage. The man wears a stylish traveling cloak of red with intertwined dragons, the elemental creature of fire, in golden-orange on the back of his cloak. His face is hidden from us, but his head appears to turned towards the castle—his ultimate goal. The castle classically represents the reward that waits for you after your quest for knowledge and advancement is completed. But we have to wonder...will he make it the rest of the way with such a heavy burden to carry? The blue sky and pretty clouds show that his environment has nothing to do with his predicament; he has chosen to carry this burden all at once and on his own.

Meanings

When the Ten of Wands appears in a reading, it is a heads-up that you have taken on too many things at the same time. Your routine and activities have become too much for you to manage. While you may enjoy wearing many hats and having an active social life, currently you are feeling overwhelmed with the demands from work, family, and/or your coven members. The bundle of ten hawthorn wands in this particular card actually represents too much of a good thing. While your intentions may have been noble, there is an overabundance of creative energy, and you are being pulled in too many different directions. You will need to let something go. Set down some of those wands in order to complete your tasks and goals with grace. Learn to delegate in the business world, your personal life, and your coven or you will have trouble successfully completing your goals.

Keywords: Many commitments, not enough time. Feeling overwhelmed and carrying too much of a burden. You need to pick and choose; what can be set aside and what is vital?

Reversed: Psychic overload, physical exhaustion. Oppression. A burden that may break you.

Page of Wands

The young Page of Wands is traveling. In the background we can see mountains and a bright blue sky. He is a young teenage boy with dark red hair and gray eyes. He wears sturdy traveling clothes, a soft golden tunic and a bright red traveling cape. The element of fire is represented by the warm colors of his clothes and his golden pendant. Around the page's neck is a large medallion in the shape and colors of a sunflower. In his right hand he holds a blooming and beribboned hawthorn wand like a walking stick. His left hand is up and cupped to the far side of his face as if he is shouting out a call. The page's expression shows us that he is bellowing for all he is worth. He is a news bearer and takes his job seriously and performs it with gusto. The Page of Wands brings enthusiasm and happiness wherever he appears. Accompanying him on his travels is an orange tabby cat. The tomcat is his familiar and trots alertly along with the page. Cats are classically associated with the element of fire, and this wise orange tabby is a fitting companion for our page as he travels abroad and shares his good news. The sunflower is associated with solar magicks, success, and fame. The clumps of ivy on either side of the Page of Wands and his familiar symbolize good luck and ward off negativity.

Meanings

This is an auspicious card and a cheerful one. When the Page of Wands announces himself into a reading, be prepared for happy news and exciting times. Typically this news will come from a younger person. Watch for a young, fair-haired person. The

Page of Wands may be announcing a new job opportunity or a promotion, or he may be heralding the impending birth of a child (especially if the Ace of Cups also appears in the spread). Expect an invitation or an opportunity.

The Page of Wands eagerly shouts out this message to you: it's time to use your imagination and your determination to achieve your goals of success.

> *Keywords:* Eagerness, a news bearer. Expect exciting and happy news soon, typically from a younger person. Determination and imagination. An invitation or an opportunity.

> *Associated Elements:* Fire and earth. Fire is the suit of wand's related element, while all four of the pages are associated with the practical element of earth.

> *Reversed:* Workplace gossip. Rumors and innuendo. Bad news.

Knight of Wands

The Knight of Wands is confident and high-spirited and coming straight towards you. He wears golden armor and is riding a white horse at full gallop. In the knight's right hand is a tall blooming wand of hawthorn, and a red streamer from the wand snaps out in the wind. The knight's helmet has the visor flipped up so we can see his face and a bit of his pale blond hair. He is fearless, and his expression is intense and passionate. The Knight of Wands wears a flowing bright red cape on his adventure, and that cape is streaming behind him. In the background we see a pretty summer sky at sunset, a lake, and three mountain peaks.

The heraldic lion design on both the knight's tunic and his horse's parade cloak symbolizes bravery and strength. The lion itself is classically associated with the element of fire, and the red and gold colors of his costume are another nod to the element from where he draws his passion and sense of daring. The Knight of Wands is a symbol of speed, adventure, and action.

Meanings

When the Knight of Wands comes roaring into your life, he brings change, exciting activity, and exhilaration. This is the card of movement; expect the unexpected. You may find yourself moving to a new job or moving to a new house. An opportunity for travel may present itself. The travel may be for business, as the suit of wands is often related to career and business. This card heralds a time of energy, bold moves, action, and adventure. This court card may also announce that an energetic, fiery, opinionated, and enthusiastic young man with fair hair and pale eyes is about to enter your life, so be on your toes.

The Knight of Wands's challenge is to embrace change, have an adventure, and enjoy the journey.

Keywords: Adventure, change, confidence, enthusiasm. Passion. Travel for business. Make a bold move now. Movement. A new job, a new house.

Associated Elements: Fire and fire. Fire is the suit of wands' related natural element, while all four of the knights are associated with the energetic element of fire.

Astrological Association: Sagittarius.

Reversed: Haste, taking dangerous risks. Confusion, a disrupted or derailed project.

Queen of Wands

The Queen of Wands reclines on her stylized sunflower throne. She has pale blue eyes and bright red, curling long hair. The queen wears a golden crown with red rubies. This charming and cheerful queen holds a tall blooming hawthorn wand in her right hand. Red streamers trail down the wand. She is surrounded by a suggestion of flames that visually link her to the fiery element that she draws her powers from. This queen draws you in by the force of her personality. She is the comforting mother, generous friend, passionate lover, and capable, sophisticated, and clever ruler all rolled into one. The Queen of Wands has on a bright yellow, square-necked gown with a red trim around the bottom of the bell-like, flowing sleeves. Around the queen's throat is a rich necklace of gold and oval-cut rubies. The rubies the queen wears in her crown and around her throat bestow energy and passion, two qualities the fiery Queen of Wands has in abundance. In the crook of her left arm is small bouquet of orange and yellow sunflowers with warm brown centers; green stems and a few heart-shaped leaves can be seen. In the language of flowers the sunflower announces confidence and flamboyance. In magickal herbalism the sunflower is worked into spells for success and fame. In the queen's lap her familiar, a fluffy orange tabby cat, is holding court and appears to be on the verge of a nap.

Meanings

When the Queen of Wands appears in a reading, brace yourself. This is where the fun begins. The Queen of Wands is all about energy, enthusiasm, and passion. This card often symbolizes a fair woman with pale eyes who loves her home, family, and pets. She is sassy, fun, warm, affectionate, and mischievous. She is the ultimate multitasker and is often involved in several groups or committees. She is intense and passionate but with a good sense of humor. It takes a lot for this woman to lose her temper—but once she does, it is an awesome force of nature. This card denotes a fire-sign woman, a talented Witch, and a natural-born leader. The Queen of Wands makes a skilled coven high priestess or energetic magickal community leader.

The message from the Queen of Wands is this: home, family, magick, and career—you can have it all. Just allow your passion for life and your creative and spiritual energy to fill you up and lead the way.

Keywords: A fire-sign woman. A woman who is generous with her affections and successful with her family, home, and career. A talented Witch and natural leader of a magickal group. The ultimate multitasker. Popular, outgoing, fun loving, charming, cheerful, classy.

Associated Elements: Fire and water. Fire is the suit of wands' related natural element, while all four of the queens are associated with the emotional element of water.

Astrological Association: Aries.

Reversed: Stubbornness, anger. A manipulative woman. Promises made but not kept. An individual who loves to create conflict.

King of Wands

handsome middle-aged man with titan-colored hair sits on a golden throne. His pale blue eyes are direct, and he is smiling just a bit. The King of Wands is leaning towards you, full of enthusiasm, energy, and generosity. He is interested and wants to be a part of your plans and goals. The King of Wands wears a regal red tunic with a golden rampart lion on the chest. In heraldry the lion represents royalty, courage, and power.

His cape is exquisite, as befits a king, and in flame colors. His crown is large, golden, and inset with rubies. In crystal magick rubies are used to sharpen the mind and intensify awareness. Around his chest drapes a livery collar, or chain of office, also made up of the solar gold and set with rubies. In his right hand he holds a tall blooming hawthorn wand. Red streamers trail down from the wand.

In the background the sky is bright yellow and red, as if the sun is rising, showing all of the fresh possibilities of the new day. This particular king rules with authority, passion, honesty, integrity, and generosity. As correctly depicted in his card, the king has a hard time staying on his golden lion throne. He is a man of action and is at his best when he is thinking on his feet and in the thick of things.

Meanings

When the King of Wands turns up in a reading, watch for a fair fire-sign man. A business man—a leader, a mover, and a shaker—he is outgoing, direct, charming, and confident. This is the man who can do it all—a "super dad." He has a successful career, coaches his kids' Little League team, and keeps his marriage vital all at the same time. This man is happiest when he is involved in many activities all at once. He is faithful, dependable, and passionate, and if he gets frustrated or annoyed, he may have to work hard to hold on to his temper. This card also represents creative expression and the championing of another's ideas and dreams. You may find that an investor or partner for your future venture is much closer than you think, or that you yourself may be the energetic supporter of another. Creativity and artistic talents are at an all-time high.

The lesson of the King of Wands is that energy and enthusiasm will help you achieve your artistic and creative goals. Be generous and supportive to the people in your life.

Keywords: A fire-sign man. A super dad. A mover and a shaker. A person who is charming, outgoing, energetic, and generous. Mentoring another. Enthusiasm, artistic expression, creativity.

Associated Elements: Fire and air. Fire is the suit of wands' related natural element, while all four of the kings are associated with the wise and thoughtful element of air.

Astrological Association: Leo.

Reversed: Arrogance, greed. Taking credit for someone else's hard work or ideas. A self-centered individual.

Pentacles

In ancient times the pentacle meant "life" or "health."
It is still the sign of the earth element
in the tarot suit of pentacles.

BARBARA G. WALKER

The suit of pentacles symbolizes the element of earth and all the magickal associations that grow from this element: the power and magick of nature, prosperity, and security. Pentacle cards flourish and grow alongside a path to understanding through work, stability, and security. This suit illustrates the influence of natural magick, the enchanting beauty and power of nature, stable relationships, loving homes, and practicality. It explores the outcome or the results of the finished creation, and pentacles represent manifestation. Pentacles signify constancy and the five physical senses of the material world that we exist within.

The suit of pentacles is linked to people born under a earthy zodiac sign: Taurus, Virgo, and Capricorn. Physically the court cards of the pentacles suit represent people that have rich and dark skin tones with brown- or hazel-colored eyes. Individuals who are drawn to the pentacles suit may be down-to-earth, be sensual, share an affinity with the natural world, and be practical and grounded. They are nurturers, generous hosts, and homemakers in the best possible sense of the word.

Ace of Pentacles

large, golden, upright, interwoven golden pentacle hovers in midair. The sky in the background is a rosy color of dawn, and golden and pink clouds are behind the pentacle. The precious golden pentacle has a leafy pattern on its surface, and the pentacle itself is surrounded by intertwined and blooming honeysuckle vines from the garden. Honeysuckle is a tenacious blooming vine aligned to the element of earth and the planet Jupiter. It is a powerful herb used in prosperity and good-luck spells, which makes it very appropriate for being featured in this earthy suit. The blooming honeysuckle flowers are symbols of new and sweet opportunities. One of the more positive cards in the tarot deck, this is a card of prosperity, fertility, wealth, stability, and growth. It also symbolizes the positive and current manifestation of your magick in the physical world.

Meanings

The Ace of Pentacles is the most potent and pure form of the feminine element of earth. This ace shows us all of the bounty that the suit of pentacles represents. Be creative, and put those blossoming ideas into action to achieve material success. Because the pentacle is hovering in midair, this card traditionally symbolized that money may just manifest in your life as if out of thin air. This card may represent a gift or an out-of-the-blue opportunity that lands in your lap. However, on a more down-to-earth note, this card—being the purest form of the earth element—reminds you to stay grounded and to use your common sense. That practicality and good judgment will guide you and your magick to success. This card often illustrates a desire to help other people on both a mundane and a magickal level. The Ace of Pentacles signifies an abiding, deep affection for the beauty of nature and a talent for green magick.

> **Keywords:** Wealth, abundance, health, happiness, security, good fortune. Love of nature, green magick, and herbalism. Magick manifested in the physical world. The element of earth.

> **Reversed:** A delay to expected income. Greed, problem with finances, failure of spellwork. Lack of faith in your own magickal talents.

Two of Pentacles

A young man is juggling two golden pentacles. He is dressed in earthy shades of green and brown, a visual link to the element of earth. The golden pentacles he juggles are in midair and above his outstretched hands. The two pentacles are inside the loops of a horizontal infinity symbol, the same lemniscate symbol from the Magician and the Strength cards. The young man has his eyes closed as if he is so skilled at juggling that he does not even need to look at those pentacles. The Two of Pentacles shows us a happy, easygoing person. It does not matter what environment he finds himself in, he can always find a way to juggle things around and to make it work. In the background behind the young man are bright blue skies, puffy fair-weather clouds, the sea, and a ship navigating the waves and currents. Even though the waters are choppy, that ship is streaming along. This is a nudge to remind you to do the same.

Meanings

When this card is tossed into a reading, it symbolizes that it is time to develop new skills. However, this will not be an issue for you, as you are adept at juggling several things at once, with ease and enjoyment. This card also illustrates that you possibly have a choice to make about two different material things. This is the card of second chances or perhaps of taking on a second job; the Two of Pentacles is the ultimate multitasking card. Finally, this card can also indicate a time to be careful with money. Watch your personal finances, and balance your budget.

Keywords: Multitasking. Second chances, second job. Keep an eye on your personal finances. Balance your budget.

Reversed: Feeling overwhelmed. Lack of concentration. Overdrawn bank account.

Three of Pentacles

A sorcerer's apprentice wearing an earthy green patterned shirt sits thoughtfully at an old wooden desk. Behind him, set in a stone wall, is a large, colorful, arched stained-glass window featuring three pentacles worked into the design of the glass. The studious young man holds a quill in his hand and is patiently creating an amulet on the parchment before him. The pentagram that he is drawing is a representation of the forces used for the manifestation of his magick and is a symbol for his spiritual development. Even though the young man is still an apprentice, he is using his talents wisely and creatively. The apprentice is gaining a quiet and solid satisfaction from his work and advancing his craft. On his desk are more tools of his trade: a bottle of ink, a burning green candle, a clutch of fresh herbs, and a bubbling bottle of magickal potion. An enchanted cat with emerald eyes sits companionably by his side and watches over the young man while the golden smoke from the spell candle wafts upwards. In time, the apprentice will become a master of his craft, thanks to all of his hard work and dedication.

Meanings

When the Three of Pentacles turns up in a reading, it is a notice that success will be attained through focus and hard work. This is a positive card of progress—one that reminds you that your creative talents should be put to good use. These talents will bring you success and help to supplement your income if you wish. This is the card of self-employment, and it is an apprenticeship card (hence the card's "sorcerer's apprentice" theme).

The actual apprenticeship may be a chance to learn a new career skill, or you may have an opportunity to enter a job training program. The Three of Pentacles can also represent a magickal apprenticeship. You may begin a new course of magickal study or perhaps are working towards a new degree in your coven. Your hard work will be noticed and appreciated by others. Now is the time to perfect your craft.

> *Keywords:* Hard work, employment, progress. Success through dedication. Creatively using your talents. Magickal apprenticeship and achievement.

> *Reversed:* Missed opportunities, laziness. No patience for the details. Unrewarding work.

An older man with gray hair and small, round glasses sits alone. He is dressed in elegant, rich green and gold clothes. He sits perched on the stone front steps of his pretty cottage, an arched and intricately carved wooden front door shut behind him. An herbal wreath hangs charmingly on the cottage door. The man looks a little suspicious as he hugs a golden pentacle to his chest. He hunches over another and has two more golden pentacles carefully tucked under each foot, as if he is afraid for anyone else to touch or try to take those pentacles away from him. His body language clearly shouts, "Mine!" But it makes you wonder … is the man just an old, penny-pinching miser? Could he simply be insecure and afraid? Or did he sacrifice his personal relationships in order to be successful and is now alone?

Intriguingly, hanging on the man's front door is a pretty wreath of blooming honeysuckle. This herb is often worked into prosperity spells. The wreath itself is a symbol of the changing seasons and cycles of life; it directly contrasts with the man's resistance to change.

Why does he cling so hard to those pentacles? What is he really guarding? His boundaries are up, and he does not want to come off those steps and interact with anyone. Perhaps he should listen more closely to the message from the honeysuckle in his wreath, for in the language of flowers honeysuckle blossoms represent generosity.

Meanings

When the Four of Pentacles comes knocking in a reading, it is a notice that someone is hanging onto something in an unhealthy way. Perhaps they are miserly or greedy and are holding tight to their money. Maybe they are obstinate and have withheld their emotions (possibly this last example is the case if the Hermit card shows up in the reading as well).

The Four of Pentacles card warns of a resistance to change. So now that you have confirmation, know that change is good; embrace the changes in your world. Relax and breathe. You may have accomplished your goals, but you are not enjoying them. Remember that nothing is fixed; everything is in motion. Accept this and move forward. It is time to lower your boundaries a bit. Reconnect with friends and family, and find the joy in your life again.

> *Keywords:* Resistance to change. Solitude, unhealthy boundaries. Accomplishing your goals but remaining unhappy. Obstinacy. The need to relax and accept change gracefully.

> *Reversed:* Selfishness, greed, hoarding. Overwhelming fears about money.

Five golden interwoven pentacles hang upon a barren tree. It is winter, and there is snow around the base of the tree and the hillside. The leafless branches stand out dramatically against the winter landscape. An icy-looking and cold, cloudy sky is in the background. This Minor Arcana card can symbolize that you feel shut out in the cold, away from lovers, friends, or other Witches. However, this card is all a matter of perception. For example, the blanket of snow may symbolize isolation—or, instead, it may give a fresh and clean look to an otherwise bland landscape. The snow can be a sign that it is time to make a fresh start. In the foreground a lone snowdrop flower raises its head through the snow. The snowdrop flower symbolizes renewal and consolation in adversity, which are the true messages of this card.

Meanings

When the Five of Pentacles turns up in a reading, it indicates a fallow time. The querent may be experiencing financial worries or feeling that they are isolated from others who share a similar belief system. There may be a feeling of disconnect and isolation, or they may be losing faith in themselves. There is anxiety and stress, and the focus must be turned towards working through the tough times instead of indulging in fear and feeling sorry for yourself. That snowdrop flower is significant; it shows that life goes on, and rebirth is possible. Help is available if you ask. No matter how dark or cold the winter may be, spring, growth, and new possibilities are just around the corner.

Keywords: Financial worries. Anxiety, stress, and working through the tough times. Feeling shut out or isolated. Renewal and hope in adversity.

Reversed: Loss, sadness, regret, remorse.

A kind gentleman dressed in elegant earth-colored clothes of green and bronze appears to be showering poor children with six golden pentacles. He has dark hair, a smiling face, and an emerald velvet cap with a large feather in the brim. Around his neck is a gold necklace. His cape is fur trimmed and regal. The six pentacles spill out from the man's generous hand and into the children's outstretched ones. He is clearly delighted in being able to help others less fortunate than himself. The background is bright, lush green grass and a pretty blue sky, which symbolizes a happy and prosperous moment in time. The children in the foreground are a young boy and girl. Their clothes appear a bit shabby compared to the gentleman's; however, the expressions on their faces show how delighted they are by their benefactor's generous gifts. The true lesson of this card is giving and receiving. There is a balance between these two acts. This card is more of an illustration of the positive energy that is exchanged between the gentleman and the children and less about charity.

Meanings

This is a card of generosity and of gifts received. The gift is something of value—not necessarily money. The gift may be lending someone a helping hand, your time, or your attention, or even sharing your talents. Classically this is a card of assistance and donations to a worthy cause. This "gift" may be monetary or it could be emotional support, a volunteer opportunity, or a way to give back to the community. Another meaning is gladly paying a karmic debt. This card also turns up when a scholarship is on the horizon. Abundant, positive, and prosperous energy is flowing freely at this time. It's an opportune moment for prosperity magick.

Keywords: Giving and receiving. Generosity. Freely giving of your time and talents. Volunteering or giving back to the community. Charity, scholarships, payment of a karmic debt. Prosperity energy is flowing at this time.

Reversed: Theft, feeling cheated, being swindled, feeling taken advantage of. Suspicion of another's motives.

Seven of Pentacles

A dark-haired young man stands next to a tall, lush, and green leafy plant. On the plant are seven golden pentacles. The young man rests his chin upon his crossed, gloved hands. He looks tired but satisfied as he takes a break from his gardening and leans upon a long-handled gardening tool. The young man wears practical and sturdy medieval-style clothes in earthy shades of green, yellow, and brown that are suitable for working in a garden. The sky behind him is blue, clear, and fair, and the surrounding landscape is green and lush. All of the effort, time, and work the young man has put into the care of this plant are paying off. The gardening tool that he leans upon could be a shovel buried in the soil or a hoe hidden in the lush grass—either way, it's to remind you that you have many tools available to you in your quest for success and prosperity. It's time to choose the best tool for the task, take it out, and put it to use. Invest in yourself; all of your efforts and hard work will bear wonderful fruit, just as this young gardener's has.

Meanings

When the Seven of Pentacles sprouts up in a reading, it speaks of rewards after hard work. This is the card of harvest. The rewards were well worth all of the effort you put into your goals and projects. The suit of pentacles is linked to material wealth, and it is also the suit of manifestation. Now is the time to sit back, take stock of what you have accomplished, and enjoy the fruits of your labors. Enjoy the satisfaction of a job well done.

Keywords: Harvest, reaping the fruits of your labors. Satisfaction of a job well done. Appreciation. Hard work equals abundant rewards.

Reversed: Missed opportunities. Time to start over. Disappointment.

Eight of Pentacles

A Witch sits behind a wooden work table in an alchemist's lab at twilight. She has a thoughtful expression on her face and wears a gown of leaf green with lace at the edges of her sleeves. She holds in her hands a large golden pentacle and is polishing it carefully with a cloth. Her hair is curly and wild as if she has been working diligently for some time. Her eyes are green and focused solely upon her task. On the table before her is an open grimoire, a burning candle, a piece of antler from a deer, a few clutches of fresh herbs, and a human skull. Her familiar, a raven, perches on the top of her chair and appears to be keeping an eye on the room for his mistress. Representing the mysteries of the Craft and magick, ravens are the traditional animal ally of the seer. Behind the Witch, on the stone wall alongside large mullioned windows, neatly hang seven other golden pentacles. She is almost finished and is putting the final polish on this eighth pentacle. Soon her task will be complete, and she will add the last pentacle to the other seven that are displayed so carefully upon the wall. In this card we see that the Witch cares more about the integrity of the work itself and not the glory that may come when her task is done.

Meanings

When the Eight of Pentacles turns up in a reading, it tells of a time for practical knowledge, determination, and skill. This is a moment of hands-on training or of intense study with your career or the magickal arts. Here is an opportunity to immerse yourself in a creative project such as art or writing.

Being focused, disciplined, and diligent with your project, you will put all of your skills to good use. By combining all of your gifts with hard work, there will be success. This is not a card of fame; this is a card that reminds you of how effort, focus, and creativity often bring growth, gain, and a sense of accomplishment. This card can also show up in a reading when there is a long, involved project nearing a successful completion.

Keywords: Diligence, skill, attention to detail. Study and practice of the magickal arts. Work in progress, a project that is nearing a successful completion.

Reversed: Lack of commitment. No ambition. A delay in a project's completion.

Nine of Pentacles

A Garden Witch stands smiling and alone in a lush garden under an arbor. She is surrounded by verdant foliage and flowers, and she almost seems to be dancing. Clearly she is happy, confident, and self-sufficient. The woman has brown hair and green eyes, while her velvet dress is a deep earthy brown with forest-green trim. Her powers are enhanced by being out in the garden and encircled by nature. The golden earrings she wears are a quiet nod to her success and prosperity. Around her neck is a necklace of nine green tourmaline stones. Those nine jewels are a link to the number of her card, while green tourmaline is the complementary stone of the herbalist and the magickal gardener.

Growing upon and twined within the arbor are nine large, magickal, five-petaled yellow flowers. In the center of each of these nine star-shaped flowers is a metallic golden pentacle center. A handsome falcon perches on the arbor just above the woman as if to keep her company. The falcon is her animal ally. The falcon in this card represents focus, intuition, inspiration, and confidence. In this card we learn one of the mysteries of the Craft: that interacting with nature and tending to the earth does enhance your spirituality.

Meanings

When the Nine of Pentacles blooms in your reading, it tells of a time of joy and abundance. This tarot card classically represents a person who is elegant, successful, and happiest when surrounded by beautiful things in nature. It symbolizes a Witch who taps into the element of earth to receive their powers. No matter what their title may be—Garden Witch, Green Witch, or magickal herbalist—this is an earthy, practical person who enjoys nature, makes and keeps a beautiful home, and grows a magickal garden. In addition, this card represents sharing the magick and the secrets of the garden with others. You are being called upon to connect to the earth and to study its mysteries. Finally, the Nine of Pentacles can represent that financial worries are over. It heralds a time of creative focus, confidence, and personal growth.

>*Keywords:* Garden Witch, herbal magicks, green
>magick. Happiness, success, confidence, abundance,
>self-sufficiency. Magickal powers and spirituality can
>be enhanced by getting your hands into the soil and
>tending the earth.

>*Reversed:* A lack of spiritual inspiration. Complacency.
>While you have achieved success, do not take it for
>granted; keep working and moving forward.

happy and loving couple embrace and look at their baby and the baby's grandfather in the foreground. The grandfather sits beneath a stone arch with his grandchild on his knee, and he is gazing down at the little one with love. The grandfather has a knowing smile upon his face; perhaps he is one of the Wise Ones. A glowing, bright light is passing from the elder's hand to the baby. Delighted by the light, the baby laughs up at the grandfather. This scene illustrates magickal knowledge or psychic talents that are passed down, or inherited, from your ancestors. The family's bond is solid and strong. A lovable and large family dog is trying to get some attention too and has flopped down in the grass protectively next to them. The dog is a classic symbol of loyalty and companionship.

Above the four people, ten golden, upright pentacles are shown. In the far background we see the family's large turreted home with a landscaped lawn and tidy gardens. Gardens are magickal places, and in this card it shows the lovely home's gardens are carefully tended—not unlike the relationship between the family members.

Meanings

Classically this card meant achievement, financial security, and support emotionally or perhaps monetarily from your relatives or loved ones. As the final pip card in the pentacles suit, it shows the ultimate outcome of both abundance and spirituality: a happy home and loving friends and family. By "family" I mean the strong emotional bond between a group of people who share affection. Remember that family is more than just blood relatives. Family may be your partner, your children, your friends, your pets, or your coven members. When this card turns up in a reading, the querent has a loving "family" and a happy home life. This is the card of commitment, loyalty, community, and success. This card can also symbolize legacies of a psychic or magickal talent passed down through the family tree. Magick is all around you; embrace it.

> **Keywords:** Commitment. Community and financial success. Happy and content family/coven. Support, thankfulness, loyalty. A family legacy of magick. Inherited psychic talents.

> **Reversed:** The burden of family and/or coven problems. Unsolicited and unwanted advice or interference in your personal life. A group that does not cherish you and instead smothers and controls. Conflicts coming from a will or an inheritance.

Page of Pentacles

young woman with darker skin tones, black hair, and brown eyes stands holding a large golden pentacle. She is in a garden setting and stands under a blooming magnolia tree. In the background we see a pretty blue sky and a lush landscape. The page holds up the pentacle and looks as if she is studying it most carefully. She wears a romantic spring-green gown with pink floral trim. A five-petaled flower pendant is around her throat and is a discreet pentagram. Her gown, its colors, the floral trim, and her medallion all are subtle links to the suit of pentacles' ruling element of earth. A white hind peeks from around the tree just behind the Page of Pentacles. The doe contentedly nibbles on the green grass and is the young woman's companion. Traditionally, a white hind is a faerie creature. The white hind invites you to explore the realm of the fae. This otherworldly doe symbolizes magick and miracles. The magnolia tree that blooms so charmingly in this card also corresponds to the element of earth. Finally, in the language of flowers the magnolia blossom symbolizes sweetness, beauty, perseverance, and a love of nature.

Meanings

The Page of Pentacles represents a person who is studious and quiet. They are generous, kind, and a "fixer." This page denotes not only a faithful friend but one who will work hard to achieve their goals. With focus and practical hard work, they will be very successful. This card can also symbolize a student of the magickal arts who is enthusiastic, fascinated, and completely absorbed with their studies, or a student who feels the call to explore Faery magick. Now is the time to focus on your spirituality. Take a look at how your spellwork manifests on the physical plane. If you want your magickal practice to flourish, then you must allow it time to blossom and grow.

The message of the Page of Pentacles is this: open your eyes, look to nature, and patiently study her ways to understand the lessons of earth magick that await you there.

Keywords: A time of study. Love of nature. Patience, kindness, generosity. Being drawn to the Faery realm. Enthusiasm, success. Take the time to focus on your spirituality.

Associated Elements: Earth and earth. Earth is the suit of pentacles' related natural element, while all four of the pages are also associated with the practical element of earth.

Reversed: Having a disconnect to your magick. Feeling smothered or trapped in the mundane world. Boredom, lack of focus.

Knight of Pentacles

The Knight of Pentacles is patiently sitting still while mounted on a black horse. The knight's visor is up, and he is looking carefully at the surrounding countryside. He seems friendly, but he is still just a little mysterious. The golden pentacle he carries close to his chest, like a shield, symbolizes the knight's steadfast faithfulness. The knight's armor is polished to a gleam, and he wears a grass-green tunic and a cloak. Green is the color of nature, Faery, fertility, and Witchcraft. The trim, bridle, and reins on the knight's horse all bear a green leaf motif, another visual link to the earth element.

The Knight of Pentacles is a representative of the Goddess, as is the Green Knight of myth and legend. And just like that Green Knight, the Knight of Pentacles does not actively seek out battles, but he is ready for them all the same. Note the heraldic stag on his horse's emerald parade cloak. In heraldry the stag symbolizes harmony, peace, and that the knight will not fight unless he is provoked, which makes it a perfect symbol for our Knight of Pentacles. In the background we see a yellow sky at dawn, golden and green fields, and a stream. A magnificent stag appears silhouetted against the landscape. The stag represents the element of earth and the qualities that encompass the Knight of Pentacles, such as pride, poise, and integrity.

Meanings

When the Knight of Pentacles arrives in a reading, expect a test of some kind. This will not be a drama-filled scenario but a quiet test of your honor and personal beliefs. Remember that the Green Knight of legend was a "tester" of other knights.

While he was a friendly character, he was also mysterious. In a reading, the Knight of Pentacles also represents a down-to-earth young man with a dark complexion and eyes. He is kind, compassionate, dependable, faithful, hard working, and practical. This card may also indicate that enrollment in a university, trade, or technical school is in the future. Like all of the other knight cards, the Knight of Pentacles is also a movement card, but the movement here is more methodical. This knight takes his time, actively observes, and then thoughtfully moves forward to deal with any challenges.

The challenge of the Knight of Pentacles is that active observation and methodical movement is necessary. Deal with any challenges in this way, and you will obtain a quiet victory.

> *Keywords:* A down-to-earth, practical young man. Hard work, active observation, stamina, patience, responsibility. Methodically dealing with life's challenges.

> *Associated Elements:* Earth and fire. Earth is the suit of pentacles' related natural element, while all four of the knights are associated with the energetic element of fire.

> *Astrological Association:* Virgo.

> *Reversed:* There are obstacles in your path—possibly a crossed condition. It is time to take a careful look and then methodically start to work through the situations. It will take time.

Queen of Pentacles

The beautiful and exotic Queen of Pentacles sits on her floral throne, a bower of climbing red roses growing above her. She has dark eyes, and green ribbons are worked into the braids of her raven-colored hair. Her gown is in shades of earthy green. She wears a crown made of golden leaves and set with square-cut emeralds. On the queen's forehead, she wears a red bindi. This is a symbol of the mystical third eye and of wisdom. In particular, the red color of the gems in her bindi design represent honor, love, and prosperity. As befits royalty, around her throat is a heavy, rich necklace of square-cut emeralds. The emerald is an enchanting stone that gifts its wearer with bliss and loyalty. The queen holds a golden pentacle in her right hand, and in the crook of her left arm she holds a bouquet of white and green tulips, honeysuckle, and golden wheat, bound together with pale green ribbons. Behind the queen's throne is a beautiful landscape and blue skies, while an adorable brown dog sits at her feet. The flowers the queen holds are all linked to the element of earth. Green tulips symbolize prosperity and luck in love; honeysuckle, wealth and devoted affection; and the wheat, abundance and riches. The red roses in the bower around the queen signify beauty and love. The dog corresponds to the element of earth and is a sign of loyalty and companionship.

Meanings

When the Queen of Pentacles appears in a reading, look for the ultimate earth mama. This card represents a mature woman who may have dark hair and eyes. She is practical and has a deep love of nature and a spiritual connection to the earth. While this queen is sensual, gorgeous, and loves beautiful things, she will work hard to get and maintain the things she cherishes. Gardening, cooking, or redecorating, she is always creating or tending to something or someone. This queen is happiest when she is nurturing others. She is a devoted wife and mother, an amusing friend, a generous hostess, and a passionate lover all rolled into one. The Queen of Pentacles is often linked to the Empress card. If they should both turn up in a reading, motherhood is the prime focus. The Queen of Pentacles is the definitive nurturer card. This card speaks of welcoming, cozy homes; happy families; beloved pets; loyal friends; fun; and affection.

The message of the Queen of Pentacles is to embrace your love of the beautiful things in this world. Create a beautiful and magickal atmosphere for yourself and your loved ones.

Keywords: An earth-sign woman. A homemaker in the best sense of the word. Emotional fulfillment. Generous hostess, loyal friend, nature lover, earth mama, devoted wife and partner. Hearth and home. Motherhood.

Associated Elements: Earth and water. Earth is the suit of pentacles' related natural element, while all four of the queens are associated with the emotional element of water.

Astrological Association: Capricorn.

Reversed: Obsession with possessions and material wealth. Holding appearance and social status in too high of a regard. A false friend. Suspicion, jealousy, unfaithfulness.

The handsome King of Pentacles is seated in an outdoor stone courtyard and leans back comfortably against royal purple cushions in his golden throne. He has black hair, a neat beard and moustache, and dark brown eyes, and he wears a leafy gold crown set with emeralds. The King of Pentacles holds in his left hand a large golden pentacle that he is gazing down upon. His right arm rests upon the arm of his throne, and he holds a golden scepter. The King of Pentacles wears a simple livery collar, or chain of office, of gold with emeralds. The emerald is an inspiring stone that grants patience. We see chain mail underneath this king's royal robes, which shows us that while he is a ruler, he still has the skills needed to defend his land and his people. A heraldic white stag, often called a hart, appears on the chest of the king's robe. In heraldry a white hart is a symbol of royalty. Behind the King of Pentacles, in the distance, we see a turreted castle. When castles appear in tarot cards, they show us that the quest for knowledge and advancement is complete, which is fitting for the final card in the Minor Arcana. Around the king grows a grapevine heavy with ripe purple grapes. The grapevine and grapes symbolize prosperity, plenty, and domestic happiness.

Meanings

When the King of Pentacles makes an appearance in a reading, know that with hard work and determination, success is on its way. The King of Pentacles represents a man with dark hair and deep brown eyes. He is easygoing, responsible, and, most importantly, a realistic man. An earth-sign man, he is strong, steady, and mature, and enjoys the simple pleasures in life. He is a generous and supportive personality and a loving, loyal spouse. He is a protective father who honestly enjoys his children. This man is successful, practical, and content with his life. He is a skilled craftsman and one who enjoys gardening, landscaping, farming, or woodworking. He is happiest when he is working with the soil or making something with his hands. He has worked hard and has earned his comfort and success.

The lesson of the King of Pentacles is that your efforts have manifested into success. Prosperity will be drawn to you.

> *Keywords:* An earth-sign man. Determination, hard
> work, wealth, security, success, responsibility. A skilled
> craftsman. Protector of the family. A mature individual
> who is a rock to lean on in tough situations.

> *Associated Elements:* Earth and air. Earth is the suit
> of pentacles' related natural element, while all four of
> the kings are associated with the wise and thoughtful
> element of air.

> *Astrological Association:* Taurus.

> *Reversed:* A person who is brooding, stubborn, and a
> little controlling. Materialism. Losing sight of what is
> truly important.

Tarot Spreads

*What could be more convincing, moreover,
than the gesture of laying one's cards
faceup on the table?*

JACQUES LACAN

There are many varieties of tarot card spreads, which allows for some personalization and freedom while doing your readings. There are a few classic spreads, such as the seven-card spread called the Horseshoe and the three-card reading. What you need to remember is this: the pattern that the cards are laid out in provides the structure for any reading.

However, trust your instincts. If, for example, the old Celtic Cross Spread does not resonate with you personally, then don't use it. I have created a few new witchy tarot spreads for this deck. I thought, when all was said and done, it would be best to include something new and fresh for the Witches Tarot. These readings include the Triple Goddess Spread, the Four Elements Spread, and the Wheel of the Year Spread. Each of these new readings includes a spell verse that helps fine-tune the divination.

One-Card Reading

Simplicity is the ultimate sophistication.

Leonardo da Vinci

This card reading is short, simple, and to the point. It gives you an instant answer. Shuffle the deck, and then fan the cards out facedown across the table. Say out loud, "What is it that I most need to know?" Now choose one card. You may want to hold your hand out over the cards and see which one "feels" right to you, or choose one at random. Flip the card, and there is your answer.

Other good questions for a one-card reading include:

- What is my personal lesson for the day?

- Is there a message for me from my guides or from the God and Goddess today?

- What do I need to know before I cast this spell?

- How will my spellwork manifest?

Finally, a simple, single card reading is a nice way to get a handle on whatever lessons your day may hold. Shuffle the deck, ask the gods to guide your hand and help you comprehend their message, and pull out one card. This is also fun to do at a coven gathering. Simply have each coven member pull one card and pass the deck clockwise around the circle. Discuss the meanings and talk about the cards with your coven members.

Three-Card Reading

Therefore, when the mind knows itself and loves itself,
there remains a trinity—that is the mind, love, and knowledge.

Peter Lombard

Three-card readings are fun. There are many variations on how you may interpret a trinity of cards. One of the most common three-card spreads is as follows:

1) Past

2) Present

3) Future

Or, when divining the answer to a problem or problematic situation, you can use this interpretation, where the three-card positions are defined as:

1) What is unknown about the current problem

2) What is blocking you

3) How to proceed for best results

To add some witchy flair to a three-card reading, shuffle the cards carefully, and, while you do, say the first line of the spell:

By all the power of the magick of three ...

Deal out the three cards facedown, and then say:

These cards will now reveal their wisdom to me.

Now turn the cards over and read them.

Seven-Card Horseshoe Spread

The success of a reading depends not on the facts but on its effect on the querent, its power to move and change a person in a beneficial way.

Mary K. Greer

Without a doubt, this is my favorite style of tarot reading. What is nice about this reading is that you can layer another set of cards over the first. This gives you a deeper meaning and provides more insight into a reading. Shuffle the cards well and ask your question. Deal out seven cards from left to right to create a horseshoe. Now take a careful look at the cards that appear in your reading.

- The first card of the reading, starting from the left, will signify the past and what brought you to this point.

- The second card is the present, meaning what is happening right now.

- The third card shows the future—what is yet to be.

- The fourth card represents your best course of action, or the best way for you to proceed.

- The fifth card represents the other people in the situation—who are they, what motivates them, and how they affect your life.

- The sixth card signifies your obstacles and your fears.

- The seventh and final card is the outcome card.

The Significator Card Reading

A man may not always be what he appears to be,
but what he appears to be is always
a significant part of what he is.

WILLARD GAYLIN

A significator card is a card used as a prop, or a tool, to focus upon in a tarot reading. The card typically represents the querent (the questioner or client). The significator card may also be used to illustrate the circumstances about which the guidance is being sought, such as the High Priestess card for a Witch inquiring about how to best deal with issues in her coven, or the High Priest for a gentleman who is wondering what his correct magickal path would be or where to focus his studies. Use your imagination. What other Major Arcana cards would you use as a focal point for various situations?

When a significator card is used in a reading, it is removed from the deck and placed faceup in the center of the table so it is easily seen and focused upon. The rest of the cards are shuffled and then dealt out around the significator card for various styles of readings.

If a significator card is used to represent the querent, then a court card is typically chosen on the basis of which card looks most physically like the client. Take a look at the following court card significator classifications.

Physical Appearance for Significator Cards

The suit of cups symbolizes a person with dark blond or pale blond hair and blue or green eyes.

The suit of wands represents individuals with fair complexions, blond or red hair, and pale blue or gray eyes.

The suit of swords illustrates a person with brown hair and green, blue, or hazel eyes.

The suit of pentacles corresponds to people with dark hair, dark brown eyes, and deeper complexions.

The problem with this classification is that not every hair color and skin tone is represented, so think of the above suggestions more as guidelines than actual rules.

Court Cards as Significator Cards:
Astrological and Elemental Personalities

All human beings are interconnected,
one with all other elements in creation.

HENRY REED

You can use the different characters within the court cards to fine-tune your significator card even more: use pages for children, knights for young adults, and queens and kings for middle age and older. Furthermore, you can link the significator card to the querent's astrological sign, or do as I do and use their elemental personality traits to match those up with the most complementary court card.

I find that it works like a charm!

Astrological Signs
for Significators

Cups: Cancer, Scorpio, and Pisces (Water)

Wands: Aries, Leo, and Sagittarius (Fire)

Swords: Gemini, Libra, and Aquarius (Air)

Pentacles: Taurus, Virgo, and Capricorn (Earth)

Elemental Personality Traits
for Significators

Mystical, empathic, and emotional? Water—Cups

Clever, cerebral, and witty? Air—Swords

Fiery, passionate, and outgoing? Fire—Wands

Earthy, practical, and easygoing? Earth—Pentacles

Finally, when choosing a significator card, I tend to use the page cards for young people, the queens for women, and the kings or knights for men. I let my instinct and intuition guide my hand and my choice. For example, if I were doing a reading for a woman, I would look carefully at the person I was doing the reading for and then choose whichever one of the four queen cards were most like her personality.

The Triple Goddess Spread

Listen to the words of the great Mother…

Doreen Valiente

I came up with the idea for this Triple Goddess reading as Mark, the artist, was working his way through the illustrations of the Major Arcana. I had been explaining the concept of the Triple Goddess to him as he finished the High Priestess card. I told him that the High Priestess card, in fact, represented the Maiden, while the Empress card was the Mother aspect of the Goddess. He commented with a chuckle that that must be why I had insisted on her being obviously pregnant in the illustration. As I explained how the third aspect was the Crone Goddess, we ended our conversation, since I had a different book to finish and he had a lot of tarot illustrations to work on.

I was going over my notes on the script that had been written a year previously, and I kept being drawn to the illustration guidelines I had written for the Moon card. It just didn't seem right. It was very classic, with the Crone's face in the waning moon, but it didn't really inspire me. As I love classic tarot images, I was unsure of what to do, so I decided to let the idea brew for a while. I had a few days before Mark would tackle that particular card anyway, so I got ready to run some errands instead.

I tossed on a T-shirt, which happened to have the Triple Goddess illustrated on it; I caught my reflection in the mirror, and then it hit me: as a Witches' deck, there was no better reason than to make the Triple Goddess a vital part of the deck. The Moon card was my opportunity for a better interpretation of the Crone.

I had one deity in mind: one of my favorites, Hecate. I called Mark back and then we brainstormed. I made some changes to my script for that card and sent him some reference images. He loved the idea of Hecate and that we would push that particular card beyond what was average or expected—just like Hecate herself.

I felt the Goddess was looking over my shoulder that day, and with images swirling in my mind of what I imagined the Crone's card to become, I sat down at my desk and wrote in a spiral notebook the Triple Goddess reading. Here is the layout.

This reading uses three significator cards: the High Priestess for the Maiden, the Empress for the Mother, and the Moon for the Crone. Place these three cards in a row and then shuffle the remaining cards carefully. Ask the Triple Goddess to share her wisdom with you. Repeat this charm:

Maiden, Mother, and Crone, now guide my hand and heart.
Show me your wisdom today by this Witch's art.
With the power of three times three,
As I will it, so shall it be.

Now deal three cards under each aspect of the Goddess. You will have nine cards in all.

- The Maiden shows you the possibilities—your hopes and dreams and what yet may be.

- The Mother shows you how your projects and goals have come to fruition and what is happening right now.

- The Crone shows you the outcome and your karma—the things that are unseen and what you may be unaware of or afraid to face.

The Four Elements Spread

Earth and water, air and fire,
wand, pentacle, and sword...

DOREEN VALIENTE

This spread works with four significator cards: all of the aces. As the aces classically symbolize the unity and perfection of each of the four natural elements, choosing the aces as focal points for this spread made perfect sense to me.

To begin, remove all of the aces from the deck. Arrange them with the Ace of Pentacles (earth) on the top, the Ace of Swords (air) to the right, the Ace of Wands (fire) at the bottom, and the Ace of Cups (water) to the left.

Take a moment to ground and center and contemplate the power of each of the elements and what they bring into your life. Ask the elements to help guide you along your path.

Repeat this charm:

Elements of earth, air, fire, and water,

Assist me now, and lend me your great power.

Let your magickal energies swirl quickly around,

Allowing strength, wisdom, courage, and love to be found.

May the messages in these cards show me the way

So I can walk my path with wisdom every day.

Now shuffle the remaining cards and ask what lessons you need to learn from each of the elements. Deal one new card from the deck next to each of the element cards.

- The earth (pentacles) card shows you what you need to be grounded, strong, and prosperous.

- The air (swords) card illustrates what you need for knowledge and clear communication.

- The fire (wands) card announces what is required for success, courage, and passion.

- The water (cups) card whispers what is needed to bring forth loving emotions and healing.

Magickal Variations: If you like, you can add the Magician card to the center of the circle of aces. Visually this will increase the focus and the power of the spread. Remember, the Magician has all four of the Minor Arcana symbols upon his altar. This Major Arcana card is a perfect portrayal of an individual who works harmoniously with the powers of the four elements and wisely with nature.

Should you decide to add the archetypal imagery of the Magician to the four elements spread, insert these lines at the end of the previous charm as a tagline:

As above, now so below,
Around the Magician the answers will flow.

The Wheel of the Year Spread

May you be blessed with peace and safety in all four seasons.

CHINESE PROVERB

For this spread you will pull the Wheel of the Year card from the deck. Use this as the significator, and place it in the center. Shuffle the remaining tarot cards and then, in a clockwise pattern, deal out eight cards around the central significator card.

Take a moment to ground and center and to contemplate the power and mysteries of each of the eight sabbats. To help you focus and interpret the card spread, repeat this charm:

> *The Wheel of the Year Spread has wisdom true to share,*
> *Enlighten me as I seek to know and to dare.*
> *Eight cards, one for each of the Witches' holy days of the year,*
> *Show me the correct way to travel so my path may be clear.*

Of the eight cards dealt around the significator card, their order is up to you. However, I typically make the top card represent the next sabbat to occur in the year. In other words, if you are doing this spread in late July, then the next sabbat is Lughnasadh, so Lughnasadh would be the first card at the top of the circle. Going clockwise to its right would be the card for the Autumn Equinox, then continuing around clockwise, the next card would represent the lessons for Samhain, Yule, Imbolc, the Vernal Equinox, Beltane, and Midsummer.

Magick with the Witches Tarot Deck

There is magic, but you have to be the magician.
You have to make the magic happen.

Sidney Sheldon

I heartily encourage you to employ the Witches Tarot cards in your spellwork. Tarot cards make wonderful tools for spellcasting, as they can become neat and clever visual guides. Not only does this practice give you something magickal and attractive to focus on, it will help you to build a relationship with the cards themselves. The cards in the Witches Tarot deck make great props in ritual, and—best of all—you have seventy-eight of them with which to work your witchery!

Recently I taught a class on the four elements and personal power. I had set up a pretty elemental altar for the students to see when they arrived. There were fresh flowers from my garden scattered across the altar, and each corner of the table was dedicated to one of the four elements. There were crystals for earth, shells for water, feathers for air, and a red, cinnamon-scented candle for fire. My students were surprised to see that I had included the ace of each tarot suit at the appropriate point of the altar as well. I explained the symbolism and then stood there grinning as I watched the wheels in their brains start to turn... As the four aces personify the basic elemental quality of their suit, they actually make wonderful elemental representations during magick. Try it out sometime. Be creative—see what you can conjure up!

You may decide to add candles or other accessories to these tarot spells. I kept these spells basic, with plenty of room for personalization. As I have said many, many times, personalizing the spells—adding a bit of yourself into the ritual—makes your witchery unique and thereby more powerful.

Court Cards for Personal Magick and Meditation

For something different, consider using your Witches Tarot cards as a focal point in meditation and personal magick—for example, if you were beginning a new project and needed to be inspired or if you needed help meeting a looming deadline. If you could really could use a burst of enthusiasm and energy for that project, then pages are perfect to work with.

Calling on the Pages for Inspiration and Enthusiasm

To begin, place the appropriate page at a each quarter: pentacles in the north, swords in the east, wands in the south, and cups in the west. You may cast a circle or just roll with it; either way, circle or no, will work out just fine. Then stand in the center of the cards and say:

May the pages' enthusiasm surround me today,

May I be blessed with their sense of adventure, come what may.

By the four suits of pentacles, swords, wands, and cups,

May this magick circle surround and boost me up!

Now take a seat; stay in the circle and meditate. If you like, you can turn and face each card, pick them up, and look at them closely. Study each of the pages, and see what sort of inspiration comes your way. When you have worked your way around and contemplated all four of the pages, ground and center yourself, and then close the spell with the following lines:

For the good of all, with harm to none,

By tarot's magick, this spell is done!

If you did cast a circle, open it now. Return the cards to your deck, and get to work on that project! You will find the enthusiasm of the four pages to be most inspiring. (I had a hard time keeping up with them as I finished this book!)

Other Spellcasting Options with Court Cards

Consider working with the four kings for powerful and wise magick—when you could use a little extra wisdom or reaffirm your integrity. The four queens are wonderful for emotional, creative, and compassionate varieties of magick. Likewise, the four knights are impressive when it comes to dealing with challenges, change, and movement. All you need to do is follow the basic spell outline.

Here are the spell verses for working with the four kings, queens, and knights. To begin, place the appropriate court card at a each quarter: pentacles in the north, swords in the east, wands in the south, and cups in the west. You may cast a circle or not; either way, circle or no, will work out just fine. Then stand in the center of the four cards and repeat the appropriate verse.

. . . .

Kings' Verse

The authority of the four kings will inspire me today,
May I be blessed with wisdom and integrity throughout my day.
By the four suits of pentacles, swords, wands, and cups,
May this magick circle around and lift me up!

. . . .

Queens' Verse

May the queens' loving inspiration surround me today,
May I be blessed with their strength and compassion come what may.
By the four suits of pentacles, swords, wands, and cups,
May this magick circle surround and lift me up!

. . . .

Knights' Verse

The knights' action and courage will move me forward today,
I'll be victorious with challenges that come my way.
By the four suits of pentacles, swords, wands, and cups,
May this magick circle surround and boost me up!

After the chosen verse is spoken, take a seat. Stay in the circle and meditate. If you like, you can turn and face each card, pick it up, and look at it more closely. Study each of the queens or knights in turn and see what sort of inspiration comes your way. When you have worked your way around and contemplated all four of the cards, ground and center yourself. Then close the spell with the following lines:

For the good of all, with harm to none,

By tarot's magick, this spell is done!

If you did cast a circle, open it now. Return the cards to your deck.

Tarot and Witchery

In these spells, I list the tarot cards along with their keywords so you can see how they all link together and why they were chosen for the specific spell. I also have suggested a coordinating candle color, crystal, and herb; just a small sprig of the herb will do. Add these accoutrements to any tarot spells when you'd like to give your witchery a bit more oomph!

Basic Directions

For all of the following tarot spells, lay out the cards in the order they are listed. If you choose, you may add the suggested colored candle, crystal, or herb. Arrange the cards, light the candle, and repeat the spell verse.

Leave the cards, crystal, and herb in place for as long as the candle burns. (Be sure to keep an eye on that spell candle!) Then, when the candle is spent, return the cards to the deck and pocket the crystal. If you added a sprig of herb to the spell, you may keep that with you or return it neatly to nature. Blessed be.

Tarot Spell to Enhance Magickal or Tarot Studies

The Magician: As above, so below. Skill, determination, connection, confidence. Strength of will. Working magick with the four elements and the elemental spirits. The Hermetic Principle of Correspondence. Elemental magick and personal power.

Three of Pentacles: Hard work, employment, progress. Success through dedication. Creatively using your talents. Magickal apprenticeship and achievement.

Eight of Pentacles: Diligence, skill, attention to detail. Study and practice of the magickal arts. Work in progress, a project that is nearing a successful completion.

Suggested Accessories: Candle color—yellow, for knowledge. Crystal—quartz, to enhance personal power. Herb—sage, for wisdom.

Spell verse:

The Magician tells us "As above, so below,"
While the apprentice works hard as a candle glows,
The Witch shows focus as she attains her magickal dreams,
Combine all these three lessons, and success will be my theme.
For the good of all, with harm to none,
By tarot's magick, this spell is done!

Tarot Spell to Create a
Strong, United Coven or Circle

Nine of Cups: Hospitality, community, graciousness. Gatherings, festivals. A wish will be granted. Enjoyable celebrations with family, coven, and friends.

Three of Cups: A happy occasion. A gathering of friends, family, or coven members to celebrate. The power of three and the magick of manifestation. Observing the sabbats, sharing experiences. Magickal advancement, psychic growth, the bonds of a healthy magickal friendship. Growth, success, creativity.

Four of Wands: Celebration, rejoicing over a happy event. Freedom, parties, baby and bridal showers, sabbat celebrations. Fertility, creativity, freedom of expression.

Suggested Accessories: Candle color—silver, for the Goddess. Crystal—moonstone, for creating an emotional bond. Herb—pink roses, for friendship.

Spell verse:

The Nine of Cups shows community and celebrations,
The Three of Cups toasts to sisterhood with a spring libation.
The Four of Wands evokes joy and the elements, one and all.
Our coven stands united through winter, spring, summer, and fall.

For the good of all, with harm to none,
By tarot's magick, this spell is done!

Tarot Spell for Abundance

Ace of Pentacles: Wealth, abundance, health, happiness, security, good fortune. Love of nature, green magick, and herbalism. Magick manifested in the physical world. The element of earth.

King of Pentacles: An earth-sign man. Determination, hard work, wealth, security, success, responsibility. A skilled craftsman. Protector of the family. A mature individual who is a rock to lean on in tough situations.

Six of Wands: Victory, achievement. Recognition for a job well done. Compliments and success. Accomplishment after hard work.

Suggested Accessories: Candle color—green, for prosperity. Crystal—aventurine, for good luck. Herb—honeysuckle, for abundance and wealth.

Spell verse:

The Ace of Pentacles is nestled in a honeysuckle vine,
The King of Pentacles complements this spell with success that shines.
The Six of Wands means triumph; my goals will surely be achieved,
Now these energies spin around, in this magick I'll believe!
For the good of all, with harm to none,
By tarot's magick, this spell is done!

Tarot Spell for Protection

Nine of Wands: Stamina, courage, protection. Be alert to trouble. Protect yourself and your reputation. Stand strong, be on guard. Magickal protection work may be required.

The Moon: The Crone aspect of the Goddess. Waning moon magick. Protection magick. Seeing through what others would keep hidden. Intuition and the development of psychic powers. Wisdom gained through years of life experiences.

The Chariot: Willpower, ambition, focus, drive. Leadership abilities. Tap into your personal power to see your magick manifest. Overcome adversity and any obstacles in your path. Don't give up; hang in there!

Suggested Accessories: Candle color—black, to banish negativity. Crystal—black tourmaline, for protection. Herb—hydrangea blossom, to break hexes.

Spell verse:

> *I stand ready to defend myself with dignity and grace,*
> *I call for protection by the Triple Goddess, Hecate.*
> *The Chariot helps me overcome obstacles in my way,*
> *This true magick encircles me now and lasts both night and day.*
> *For the good of all, with harm to none,*
> *By tarot's magick, this spell is done!*

Tarot Spell for Attracting Romance

The Fool: Follow your bliss. Adventure, fresh starts, exploration, a journey. New ideas; take a chance and chase your dreams. The beginning of a spiritual quest; exploring a new magickal path or tradition. A leap of faith.

Two of Cups: Romance. An engagement, handfasting, wedding, or reconciliation. A partnership. Equality and true love.

The Lovers: Sexual love, beauty, a romantic relationship. Decisions, commitment. Choices to be made. The choice you make now will affect your future. Love heals.

Suggested Accessories: Candle color—hot pink, for fun and affection. Crystal—rose quartz, for soft, romantic emotions. Herb—red rose, the flower of romance and passion.

Spell verse:

The Fool encourages us to dream big and take a chance,
While the Two of Cups whispers that romance is its own dance.
The Lovers card reminds us that choice shapes our destiny,
May I find someone that is loving and correct for me.
For the good of all, with harm to none,
By tarot's magick, this spell is done!

Tarot Spell to Heal a Broken Heart

Three of Swords: Delay, personal betrayal, loss. A time of drama and tears. Sadness, conflict. A spell that has backfired.

The Hanged Man: Initiation, transitional phase of life. Relax and let changes come. New outlook on life, rune magick, gaining a new perspective on a current situation.

The Star: The Star Goddess. Healing, inspiration, intuition, renewal. Hope, peace, wishes granted. Astrological magick. Wisdom. Creativity is flowing.

Suggested Accessories: Candle color—soft pink, for happiness and self-love. Crystal—bloodstone, for healing. Herb—red carnation, for restoring energy and encouraging healing.

Spell verse:

> *Three of Swords shows, though brokenhearted,*
> *my healing needs to begin,*
> *During this transition I will gain insight,*
> *the Hanged Man's wisdom.*
> *My healing starts today; negative feelings I now release.*
> *The Star card grants hope, rebirth, emotional healing, and peace.*
> *For the good of all, with harm to none,*
> *By tarot's magick, this spell is done!*

Tarot Spell for Hearth and Home

The Empress: The Mother aspect of the Goddess. Bringing new ideas into existence. Feminine power, love, sexuality, motherhood. Fertility, birth, creativity. Hearth and home, protecting love in your life, full moon magick. The power of nature.

Queen of Pentacles: An earth-sign woman. A homemaker in the best sense of the word. Emotional fulfillment. Generous hostess, loyal friend, nature lover, earth mama, devoted wife and partner. Hearth and home. Motherhood.

Ten of Cups: Love, imagination, fulfillment. Joy, good humor, happy family. Good home life, comfort and joy. Friendship, happy coven, being a part of the magickal community.

Suggested Accessories: Candle color—brown, for its grounding, earthy, and homey qualities. Stone— holey, excellent for hearth and home magick. Herb— cinnamon, for energy and protection.

Spell verse:

The Empress will surround my home with love, magick, and peace,
While the Queen of Pentacles brings comfort within my reach.
The Ten of Cups brings fulfillment and a happy family,
My home shimmers with charm and joy from this tarot witchery.
For the good of all, with harm to none,
By tarot's magick, this spell is done!

Bright blessings on your witchery and your tarot readings!

Final note: If you enjoyed this spells section of the *Witches Tarot Companion* book, you will find a dozen more enchanting tarot spells in *Book of Witchery,* one of my previously published books.

Appendix I

Minor Arcana Number and Court Card Meanings

When One made love to Zero,
Spheres embraced their arches and
prime numbers caught their breath.

RAYMOND QUENEAU

Ace: Basic elemental quality. Represents the beginning of things, new ideas, projects, or birth.

Two: The relationship between two people or principles. Reflection, harmony, and balance.

Three: Full expression of the element. Love, expectancy. The concept of creation, divinity, and fate.

Four: Stability, firm foundations, structure, and order. The Four of Wands and Four of Swords are calming and steadying, while the Four of Cups and Four of Pentacles show stagnation and restriction.

Five: Loss, conflict, regret, and problems. Crisis, creating challenges, arguments, opportunity to learn something new.

Six: Balance, harmony, love, benevolence, past actions, communication, reunion, accomplishment.

Seven: Skill, victory, luck, daring, impatience, wisdom, mystery. Magickal gifts associated with each suit.

Eight: Enthusiasm, inspiration, regeneration, success, justice, reevaluation, redirection. Development or growth in future.

Nine: Limits, boundaries, melancholy. Almost finished. Achieving results and learning from previous experience. Three times three. Emotionally satisfied, contented.

Ten: New stage of development. Completion, heritage, karma. The need to go beyond limits.

Page: Children and teens, students, messengers. Undeveloped potential, risk taking, curiosity, hopefulness, exploration, study of practical matters.

Knight: Adventure, movement, progress, action, responsibility to others.

Queen: Mothering, nurturing, creativity, caring, compassion, kindness, inspiration. Deep magickal meaning of the suit.

King: Father figure, teacher, mentor, leader. Authority, responsibility, power, success. Policy, pride, stubbornness, arrogance.

Appendix II

Symbols in Tarot Cards

Nature is a temple in which living columns sometimes emit confused words. Man approaches it through forests of symbols, which observe him with familiar glances.

CHARLES BAUDELAIRE

Armor and Chain Mail: A form of defense, it symbolizes protection and strength. It is seen in the cards the Emperor, Chariot, Death, Knight of Cups, Knight of Swords, Knight of Wands, King of Swords, Six of Wands, Knight of Pentacles, and King of Pentacles.

Bench: The bench illustrates neutrality and that it is time to have a seat and mull things over. Seen in the cards the High Priest, Justice, and Two of Swords.

Birds: Higher thoughts and spiritual messages. Seen in the cards the Hanged Man, the Star, the World, Queen of Cups, Ten of Swords, Queen of Swords, and Eight of Pentacles.

Blindfolds: There are two possible definitions to blindfolds in the Witches Tarot. One, seen in the Eight of Swords, shows that the woman feels trapped—like a hostage. Her blindfold causes disorientation and keeps her unaware of her surroundings. Then we have the opposite end of the spectrum: the Two of Swords. This blindfold prevents distraction and helps her to look within. Her other senses are heightened now; what can she learn from them?

Butterfly: A classic symbol of transformation and beauty. Seen in the Seven of Cups and Ace of Wands.

Castle: Castles are often seen in the background of the cards. They represent the reward that waits for you after your quest for knowledge and advancement is completed. Seen in the Death card, Four of Swords, Eight of Swords, Ace of Wands, Four of Wands, Ten of Wands, Seven of Cups, Knight of Cups, and King of Pentacles.

Cat: The feline is associated with the element of fire and symbolizes perception, psychic powers, mystery, and Witchcraft. Domestic cats, in all their wondrous varieties, are the classic Witch's familiar. Cats grace us with their presence in the following cards: the High Priestess, Seven of Cups, Two of Wands, Four of Wands, Page of Wands, Queen of Wands, and Three of Pentacles.

Children: Children in tarot cards typically represent the following emotions: adventure, youth, energy, enthusiasm, the joy of life, legacy, and tradition. Children are seen in the cards the Fool, the Emperor, Death, the Sun, Four of Cups, Six of Cups, Ten of Cups, Six of Pentacles, and Ten of Pentacles.

Cliffs: Symbolize being at the edge of danger and the unknown. Seen in the cards the Fool, the Hermit, the Tower, Karma, Eight of Cups, and Seven of Wands.

Crow and Raven: Mystery, magick, and cleverness. The animal ally of the seer. The raven/crow graces the following cards: the Hanged Man and the Eight of Pentacles.

Deer: The deer is associated with the element of earth. Traditionally the stag symbolized pride, poise, and integrity. A stag is seen in the World and Nine of Pentacles cards, while the white hind appears in the Page of Pentacles. The white hind is a symbol of magick, miracles, and the Faery kingdom. The stag is also seen in the heraldry of the Knight of Pentacles and the King of Pentacles.

Dog: The dog is a traditional representation of the earth element. Dogs symbolize loyalty and companionship. They add their support to the following cards: the Fool, Ten of Pentacles, and Queen of Pentacles.

Dragon: A creature of the element of fire, dragons represent the oldest of magicks and passion. Dragons are seen in the Seven of Cups and Five of Wands, and are seen in the heraldry of the Six of Wands and Nine of Wands.

Dragonflies: As creatures of the air element, they symbolize illusion. Seen in the Five of Swords and Six of Swords.

Faeries: The faeries are associated with the elemental kingdom of the air and the suit of swords. They represent a deep connection to the magick of the natural world. Faeries are seen in the cards the Magician, Two of Swords, Three of Swords, Five of Swords, and Queen of Swords.

Falcons and Hawks: These birds symbolize spiritual messages. Seen in the Ace of Swords, King of Swords, and Nine of Pentacles. They are in the heraldry of the Page of Swords and Knight of Swords.

Fish and Dolphin: These water creatures symbolize communication, emotion, intuition, and creativity. They are seen on the Page of Cups, King of Cups, and Eight of Cups.

Gardens: Gardens are typically shown in the background of a scene. They are magickal places and represent where you are on your current spiritual path. Gardens are illustrated in the cards the Lovers, Three of Cups,

Nine of Pentacles, Ten of Pentacles, and the Page of Pentacles.

Globes or Orbs: These represent power over earthy matters and concerns. Seen in the following cards: the Emperor and Two of Wands.

Heraldry: Heraldry is seen in several cards in the Witches Tarot deck. Each was chosen for its elemental association and magickal symbolism. (See individual entries for a listing of the cards they appear on.) *Dragons* (fire) mean protection, valor, and a defender of treasure. *Hawks* (air) mean eagerness, impatience, and the thrill of the chase. *Lions* (fire) indicate bravery, valor, and strength. *Mermaids* (water) symbolize eloquence, loyalty, and truth. *Stags* (earth) mean strategy, peace, and harmony.

Horses: Movement and strength, also associated with all four elements of earth, air, fire, and water. A divine symbol of the God and Goddess. Seen in the Chariot, Death, the Sun, Knight of Cups, Knight of Swords, Six of Wands, Knight of Wands, and Knight of Pentacles.

House: Home is where the heart is, and when houses—from cottages to turreted grand houses—are depicted in tarot cards, they are a symbol of the magick of family, security, and hearth and home. Houses are seen in Six of Cups, Ten of Cups, Four of Pentacles, and Ten of Pentacles.

Keys: Keys are a mystical symbol of knowledge and often represent the mysteries of the Craft. Seen in the High Priest and the Moon cards.

Lakes, Ponds, and Pools: The still water of a lake, pond, or pool reflects sunlight, moonlight, or our thoughts. Seen in many of the cards, including Temperance, the Star, Ace of Cups, Two of Cups, Two of Swords, Six of Swords, Eight of Wands, and Knight of Wands.

Lemniscate: The infinity symbol, which illustrates the cyclical nature of energy. Energy is always moving and always constant. The lemniscate is seen in the Magician, Strength, and Two of Pentacles.

Lion: Strength, loyalty, courage, and restraint. Seen on the Strength and World cards and depicted in the heraldry of the Knight of Wands and King of Wands cards.

Mermaids: Elemental creatures of water. Sexuality, intrigue, and longing. Seen on Four of Cups, Five of Cups, and Seven of Cups. The mermaid is also featured in the heraldry of the Knight of Cups and King of Cups.

Moon: Represents psychic power, feminine energy, mystery, magick, and intuition. Seen on the High Priestess, the High Priest, the Chariot, the Moon, Karma, Eight of Cups, Two of Swords, and Nine of Swords.

Mountains: Mountains indicate that we must work to reach our goals and represent triumph, challenges, and endurance. Seen in many of the cards.

Ocean and Seas: Represent infinite possibilities, great depths of wisdom, mystery, something bigger and more powerful than ourselves. Seen in the Five of Cups, Eight of Cups, Page of Cups, Queen of Cups, King of Cups, Three of Wands, and Two of Pentacles.

Pentagram: The upright five-pointed interwoven star represents the elements and spirit. It is often worn as a talisman for protection and as a charm by a Witch. Seen in the Fool (on his knapsack), the Magician, the High Priest, the Wheel of the Year, the Hanged Man, the Moon, Seven of Swords, and Nine of Wands.

Pillars: Pillars represent balance. Pillars are included in classic tarot imagery to illustrate that the figure of the card is neutral or has taken the middle ground. Seen in the High Priestess, the High Priest, and Justice.

Rainbow: A classic symbol of hope, messages, miracles, and magick. Seen in Temperance, Ten of Cups, and Seven of Cups.

Rivers and Streams: Rivers are considered to be the moving force of life. They tell of journeys and of opportunities; also, they represent flowing emotions and the stream of consciousness. Streams are a softer, gentler version of the meaning of the river. Rivers and streams are seen in the Empress, Four of Cups, Six of Cups, Ten of Cups, Knight of Cups, Eight of Swords, Ace of Wands, and Knight of Pentacles.

Rose: A magickal symbol of love, enchantment, and hope. In the language of flowers, the meanings vary according to the color of the rose. In this deck we see white, red, pink, and yellow roses. *White* are for love, unity, and beauty. *Red* indicate beauty, love, harmony, and charm. *Pink* are for friendship, romance, and affection. *Yellow* are for friendship and sunshine. Roses play prominently in the Fool, the Magician, the Lovers, Strength, Two of Cups, Three of Cups, Queen of Cups, Four of Wands, and Queen of Pentacles.

Scepter: A masculine rod of power topped with an feminine orb, scepters are a symbol of sovereignty. Scepters are seen in the Empress, the Emperor, King of Cups, and King of Pentacles.

Shield: The shield is a tool of protection and was used as a sort of statement for the world to see, depending on the designs painted upon it. The shield is featured in the Empress, Knight of Swords, and Knight of Pentacles.

Ships: Ships represent travel and thoughts. Seen in the Two of Wands, Three of Wands, Six of Swords, and Two of Pentacles.

Skulls: Skulls symbolize the promise of new life, change, and transition. The skull is considered to be the seat of inspiration and intelligence. A skull is seen in Death, the Moon, and the Eight of Pentacles.

Snow: Snow may indicate isolation or being crisp, clean, and new. Seen in the Hermit and Five of Pentacles.

Staff: A more earthy type of scepter. The staff is often used by a wise man or as a tool of the traveler. Seen in the Fool, the High Priest, and the Hermit.

Stained Glass: Stained glass represents perception alchemy. Seen in the Three of Pentacles.

Star: Stars indicate hope, destiny, illumination, and astrological influences. Seen in the High Priestess, the Empress, the Chariot, the Hermit, the Star, and Eight of Cups.

Sun: The masculine side of deity. Solar magick, strength, light, and power. Seen in the High Priest, the Lovers, the Sun, Karma, and Nine of Wands.

Sunflower: A flower of the sun and the element of fire that symbolizes success, fame, and riches. Featured in the Sun, Page of Wands, and Queen of Wands.

Teens or Young Adults: A young adult or teen portrayed in a tarot card symbolizes possibilities and discovery, and they mark the beginning of a quest for knowledge about the magickal world and about themselves. Teens or young adults are portrayed in this deck as the pages.

The masculine elements of air (swords suit) and fire (wands suit) both have male pages, while the suits of cups and pentacles (water and earth, respectively) are illustrated with female pages. You will find these young people in the following cards: the Fool, Page of Cups, Page of Swords, Page of Wands, Page of Pentacles, Two of Pentacles, and Three of Pentacles.

Throne: The throne symbolizes sovereignty and power. Seen in the High Priestess, the Empress, the Emperor, Queen of Cups, King of Cups, Queen of Swords, King of Swords, Queen of Wands, King of Wands, Queen of Pentacles, and King of Pentacles.

Triple Moon: The classic Witches' symbol of the Triple Goddess, or the Maiden, Mother, and Crone. Seen in the High Priestess and on the back of every tarot card in the Witches Tarot deck.

Tulips: The tulip flower is used in prosperity magick and corresponds to the element of earth. In the language of flowers, tulips symbolize royalty and whisper of love. Tulips are seen in the Emperor, the Lovers, and the Queen of Pentacles.

Wand: A Magician's tool used to direct and focus personal power. Seen in the Magician and the Chariot.

Wand of Hawthorn: In this deck, the wand featured in the suit of wands is a blooming branch of hawthorn. Hawthorn has the elemental association of fire; also, the hawthorn is a tree of magickal power and folklore. Magickally, hawthorn blossoms are used in both protection and fertility spells. Seen in the Magician, the Wheel of the Year, and the entire suit of wands.

Waterfalls: Waterfalls signify the active and forceful flow of emotions and the stream of the subconscious—ideas and emotions that flow and change. Seen in the Empress, Three of Cups, and Four of Cups.

Waves: Waves are the movement of emotion. Seen in the Page of Cups, Three of Cups, Five of Cups, Queen of Cups, and King of Cups.

Wolf: A wolf signifies a pathfinder, leader, guide, and teacher. Seen in the Moon.

Bibliography

*A good book should leave you
slightly exhausted at the end.
You live several lives while reading it.*

WILLIAM STYROM

Almond, Jocelyn, and Keith Seddon. *Understanding Tarot.* London, England: Aquarian Press, 1991.

Amberstone, Ruth Ann, and Wald Amberstone. *The Secret Language of Tarot.* San Francisco, CA: Weiser Books, 2008.

Andrews, Ted. *Animal Speak.* St. Paul, MN: Llewellyn Worldwide, 1994.

Carr-Gomm, Phillip, and Stephanie Carr-Gomm. *The Druid Animal Oracle.* New York: Simon and Schuster, 1994.

Cunningham, Scott. *Cunningham's Encyclopedia of Magical Herbs.* St. Paul, MN: Llewellyn Worldwide, 1996.

Dugan, Ellen. *Book of Witchery.* Woodbury, MN: Llewellyn Worldwide, 2009.

———. *The Enchanted Cat.* Woodbury, MN: Llewellyn Worldwide, 2006.

———. *Garden Witchery.* St. Paul, MN: Llewellyn Worldwide, 2003.

———. *Garden Witch's Herbal.* Woodbury, MN: Llewellyn Worldwide, 2009.

Fenton-Smith, Paul. *Tarot Masterclass*. NSW, Australia: Inspired Living Publishing, 2007.

Greenaway, Leanna. *Simply Tarot*. New York: Sterling Publishing, 2005.

Greer, Mary K. *21 Ways to Read a Tarot Card*. Woodbury, MN: Llewellyn Worldwide, 2006.

Hall, Judy. *The Crystal Bible*. Cincinnati, OH: Walking Stick Press, 2003.

Laufer, Geraldine Adamich. *Tussie-Mussies: The Victorian Art of Expressing Yourself in the Language of Flowers*. New York: Workman Publishing Company, 1993.

Mangiapane, John. *It's All in the Cards: Tarot Reading Made Easy*. New York: Sterling Publishing Company, 2004.

Moore, Barbara. *Tarot for Beginners*. Woodbury, MN: Llewellyn Worldwide, 2010.

Nahmad, Claire. *Garden Spells*. Philadelphia, PA: Running Press, 1994.

Pollack, Rachel. *Tarot Wisdom*. Woodbury, MN: Llewellyn Worldwide, 2008.

———. *78 Degrees of Wisdom*. San Francisco: Weiser Books, 2007.

Skolnick, Solomon M. *The Language of Flowers*. White Plains, NY: Peter Pauper Press, 1995.

Acknowledgments

Creating a tarot deck is a long, arduous journey. It has ups and downs, with dramas, intrigue, and—believe it or not—comedy. There is nothing like combining an organized, detail-oriented Witch with a cloud-chasing genius of an artist. Mark, the art is everything I ever hoped for. It is stunning and, honestly, I will never look at clouds the same way again...

To my husband, Ken, and our adult children Kraig, Kyle, and Erin. Thanks for enthusiastically posing for cards (even when I had you holding pottery goblets, spoons for scepters, and great big scissors for swords), and, most of all, thanks for being so excited about this project and for believing in me.

There were a few other souls brave enough to stick it out with me and keep encouraging this process over the past two and a half years. These enchanting folks include Christopher, Colleen, Jenn, Joyce, Jeanne, Kina, Solstice, Tess, and, to the ladies of my coven, thank you all for your unwavering support and friendship.

Also a loving thanks to the relatives and friends who happily posed for various tarot cards: my niece Olivia and my nephews Ethan, Hunter, and Rylan; my friends Ariel, Charlynn, Dawn, Ember, Heather, Jen, and Shawna.

In addition, a few words of appreciation for my fabulous editor, Becky Zins; to Barbara Moore; and to Llewellyn's art department. To Elysia Gallo for being a sympathetic ear, and to Cheryl York for getting me connected to the two people who would help push this project to the finish line.

Finally, with gratitude, to Bill Krause and Sandra Weschcke, the champions of this deck. They never gave up on this project, nor did they allow me to. Thank you.